SMALL
BUSINESS
CYBER
SECURITY

SMALL BUSINESS CYBER SECURITY

YOUR CUSTOMERS
CAN TRUST YOU...RIGHT?

ADAM ANDERSON AND TOM GILKESON

Published by Advantage, Charleston, South Carolina.
Member of Advantage Media Group.

ADVANTAGE is a registered trademark and the Advantage colophon is a trademark of Advantage Media Group, Inc.

Printed in the United States of America.

ISBN: 978-1-59932-590-3
LCCN: 2015957493

This publication is designed to provide accurate and authoritative information in regard to the subject matter covered. It is sold with the understanding that the publisher is not engaged in rendering legal, accounting, or other professional services. If legal advice or other expert assistance is required, the services of a competent professional person should be sought.

Advantage Media Group is proud to be a part of the Tree Neutral® program. Tree Neutral offsets the number of trees consumed in the production and printing of this book by taking proactive steps such as planting trees in direct proportion to the number of trees used to print books. To learn more about Tree Neutral, please visit www.treeneutral.com. To learn more about Advantage's commitment to being a responsible steward of the environment, please visit www.advantagefamily.com/green

Advantage Media Group is a publisher of business, self-improvement, and professional development books and online learning. We help entrepreneurs, business leaders, and professionals share their Stories, Passion, and Knowledge to help others Learn & Grow. Do you have a manuscript or book idea that you would like us to consider for publishing? Please visit advantagefamily.com or call 1.866.775.1696.

TABLE OF CONTENTS

CHAPTER 6

Framework Principle 3:

CHAPTER 7

Framework Principle 4:

CHAPTER 8

Framework Principle 5:

CHAPTER 9

A NOTE FROM THE AUTHORS

When Tom and I decided that we should write a book, it was because we felt that we had discovered something we needed to share about security and how people go about it. We didn't completely understand who needed to hear about our discovery, and it wasn't until we finished getting our observations down on paper that we were able to unpack who might find it valuable. This journey has reinforced our passion around a niche of cybersecurity—cyber risk inside the supply chains of large businesses.

With the Internet of Things growing and technology becoming more and more integrated with "mundane" processes and devices, large businesses are trusting their vendors and suppliers more and more with their intellectual capital and critical business systems. In most cases, this trust is being given without the large company even realizing they are doing it, due to the complexity of environments and systems required to run a large enterprise.

We believe that Tom's experiences as an executive of corporate security and his background in the air force, paired with my experiences as an entrepreneur and a member of the supply chain of a number of large enterprises, give us an interesting enough collection of data and observations to be worth the effort to tell you good folks about it.

How Should You Read This Book?

In this book, we cover how an understanding of the National Institute of Standards and Technology (NIST) Cybersecurity Framework and a company's role in the value chain of a enterprise's business model will allow alignment between small or midsize businesses and the security needs of the large enterprise.

In other words, we help small businesses figure out how to protect themselves so they don't become *that vendor* that caused the larger enterprises they work with to be a headline in the news.

If you are a curious person and want to learn about security, you should find enough content in the following chapters to get a decent overview of the different parts of NIST. Our examples and stories should help you understand how the parts of NIST should be applied to the different parts of your company and supply chain.

If you don't have time for that, jump to the end of the book and look at Appendix A, "Twenty-Two Ways to Lock Your Company's Cyber Doors for Under 20K," which outlines the things a small and midsize company can do to help protect their customers. If you have a more complex environment and a bit of a budget, look at Appendix B, where we reference some really smart people who talk about how to increase your NIST security maturity level.

I know I speak for Tom as well as myself when I say thank you for getting this book and reading it. Our hope is that it helps increase your level of trust in the overall cybersecurity landscape of business— or at least makes you sound smarter at dinner parties. Either is a win. Enjoy.

INTRODUCTION

Is your business protected from today's cyber threats? If you don't know, then you need this book. If you're working in the world of cybersecurity, it's essential to develop a framework in order to have a shot at creating a security plan that you can actually execute.

This book can be used in two different ways—first, to provide an overall narrative of how large businesses think about cybersecurity and how that aligns with security frameworks, and second, to provide suggestions on how smaller companies can position themselves to minimize the risks they bring to those larger organizations. If you are a small to midsize business working with large enterprises, you should leave this book with a better understanding of how large companies think and what their expectations for you will be.

This book is a team effort, and I, Adam Anderson, am working with my friend and colleague Tom Gilkeson, the head of corporate security for Michelin North America, to write it.

The comments throughout this book, whether as "I" or "we," sometimes distinguished by specific examples from my company, Palmetto Security Group, or Tom's work throughout his career, are the collective result of our work together.

FRAMEWORKS FOR CYBERSECURITY

In this book, Tom and I take the lessons we've learned and the experiences we've gained through entrepreneurship and the cybersecurity field—along with those passed on to us by the businesses and people with whom we've worked—to help you tackle the huge and complex process of cybersecurity. We want you to use a framework to simplify and structure a thought process around the question, "How do I approach cybersecurity?"

There are many ways to do this. We've chosen to focus on the NIST Cybersecurity Framework, published by the National Institute of Standard and Technology. The NIST official government website states, "The Framework, created through collaboration between industry and government, consists of standards, guidelines, and practices to promote the protection of critical infrastructure. The prioritized, flexible, repeatable, and cost-effective approach of the Framework helps owners and operators of critical infrastructure to manage cybersecurity-related risk." There are other systems and other frameworks that work, but this is the one we are using as a framework for our topic.

When many of you try to bring up cybersecurity issues to stakeholders, the very first thing they might do is begin quoting the latest computer system hack they saw on CNN. They might act in very fearful ways or be resigned to live with it, like victims of circumstance, rather than taking action. Sometimes they might treat your ideas in a comical way because they're horrified by cybersecurity and use humor to cope. And sometimes you'll be treated like a superhero, flying in at just the right time to help the damsels and dudes in distress. All of these methods are ways that people deal with traumatic situations of any kind.

CHALLENGING THE SECURITY STATUS QUO

Typically, without a solid understanding and a safe place for this conversation, bad decisions are made or no decisions made at all. People at your company would rather not know about a problem than be aware of it and feel they cannot do anything about it.

Companies must learn what to do with risk. They must build solid security into their systems and ways of doing business, and they must challenge the status quo. Involving leadership and creating a call to action is often the hardest part. Once companies learn about a risk, they must learn what to do about that risk. And that begins with not being in denial in the first place.

So when a status quo is in effect, that "I've been operating this way for a while, and I'm not dead yet" attitude change becomes scary. Change becomes hard.

THE CHALLENGE

One of the very first challenges when it comes to new risk is figuring out who is going to own it. Until you have an executive decision on who is going to own the risk and be responsible for it, nothing is going to happen. The first thing you need to do is to assign an owner and have executive sponsorship supporting your decisions and advice.

At the other end of the spectrum, if you're going to accept the risk, the decision has to come from the top. Then it's your role as the security practitioner to make stakeholders aware of their decision on risk and develop plans to mitigate that risk to the best of your ability.

That plan should be presented in a way that lets everyone know this is a business decision that security is trying to recuce risk on.

It's important to present the risk and plan of action to executive management in a jargon-free way, which is how we've achieved results in the past.

As security personnel, you have to work with staff throughout your company to educate them and address the status quo. And you must find ways to make the security policies and how you go about implementing them manageable for staff, too.

HUMAN BEHAVIOR AND SECURITY RISK

Security situations come up in ways you might never expect. One example we heard recently was that the employees at one company had so many IDs and passwords to remember for their systems that they posted them on a whiteboard in the office. People were photographing in the office and tweeting pictures without realizing that all of those passwords were now tweeted to the world.

There's a dual issue in this example. One is the complicated procedures, so complicated that no one can remember them. Then, people are allowed to take pictures in the office. This might not have been an issue in the old pre-digital days, but now with Facebook and everything else, it certainly is.

At one television company we worked with, one of our roles was to protect the company's intellectual property. Several productions started to experience leaks about shows prior to their airdate. Trying to figure out what was going on, we started investigating the spoiler fan phenomenon. Someone involved in producing a TV show had gotten a new office. He'd tweeted a photo of his desk with a call sheet on it, a document with details about the production. If you zoomed in on the photo, there was all the information you needed to post spoilers on the Internet.

WHO WOULD HAVE THOUGHT?

The key takeaway with these unfortunate situations is that many companies continue to use old behaviors and old approaches to security and other issues. They are unaware that there is any reason to be aware, since they are complying with a status quo. "Hey, this is how we do business," many companies are telling themselves, ignoring the reality that the tools have changed. The ways of interacting with people have changed. The world is a different place, where a random, harmless photo about someone proud about a new office can lead to massive data leaks. Certainly not how you want your first day on the job to unfold.

At times, it's also a psychological, human behavioral component of the status quo that needs to be examined. It sounds strange, but at times the goal of many cybersecurity folks is, "How do I fix these humans?" It's not solely about technology, as many who are not in the cybersecurity field think.

As another social media security issue, how often are your employees setting up meetings with clients via their Facebook pages? Are they posting on Foursquare where they are going to be for a sensitive business lunch, allowing the chance that a competitor might purposely sit nearby and listen in? People often don't realize how public communications have become in recent years. When you're looking from a cybersecurity perspective, that's not always a good thing.

The issue we come across regarding personnel involved in cybersecurity is that we have very smart folks who really understand the technology but may not have good people skills. The ease of understanding the threats from a cyber or technology point of view doesn't necessarily translate into the ability to communicate about what you've seen. Yes, it can fit the stereotype of the so-called cyber geek and computer nerd, but it goes far beyond that, and that is among the concerns we want to address throughout this important book.

As stated above, we believe this book has two different functions. The first is to provide an overall narrative of how large businesses think about cybersecurity and how that aligns with security frameworks. The second is to provide suggestions on how smaller companies can position themselves to minimize the risks they bring into those larger organizations. If you are a small to midsize business working with large enterprises, you should leave this book with a better understanding of how large companies think and what their expectations for you will be. All of this will become a powerful arsenal for you when explaining your company's cybersecurity needs to your C-level management.

CYBERSECURITY IS BUSINESS VALUE

At the high level, you can think of this book as a translator and an organizer for IT to business line functions. It's also about security in relation to business value. What is your business trying to accomplish, and what role should security play in that? On the opposite end of the spectrum, there is such a thing as too much cybersecurity. If your cybersecurity system prevents the business from producing value, then it's too much. We want to make sure you understand the right balance for your company and how to explain that to C-level management.

Throughout 2014 and into 2015, the issue in the vast majority of high-profile corporate cyberattacks has been an employee making a mistake or being unwittingly exploited. This was the case in the Target attack, the Home Depot attack, and the attack on South Carolina Revenue Service. We've got really smart IT people who are great at securing IT infrastructure, but one of the biggest challenges right now is that the real vulnerability being exploited is the humans.

Much of this boils down to processes and procedures and accountability, not technology. How do we do what we do? Who is doing it? How do we keep track of where they're doing it and how they're doing it? And how do we verify that what we thought was being done is actually being done?

Read on as, chapter by chapter, we explain how you can become aware of these challenges and explain them in an effective way to management. We use colorful, thoughtful examples of real-life situations, demonstrating how to overcome these challenges. Security is your business, and you'll learn how to make it the business of everyone in your company.

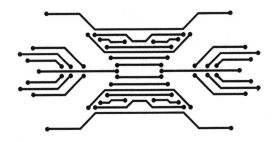

CHAPTER 1

WHY AREN'T MORE COMPANIES THINKING ABOUT SECURITY RISKS IN A CONSTRUCTIVE WAY?

When we sit down and talk through what a company's security risks are, we often refer to a company's core business model. Understanding what the business model is, what the company does, and how the company goes about doing it helps us craft security around their business functions. When we are advising a company to assess its risks, we begin by understanding how it actually makes its money and work backward from there.

Let's take retail, for example. First, retail is about supply chain—getting the products from somewhere, bringing them to a location, and presenting them in such a way that consumers can buy them. The second aspect of retail is point-of-sale: How do I perform a financial transaction for merchandise whereby somebody gets the product and I get the money for it? Understanding these fundamental truths ensures that we deal with the highest priorities.

When considering security risks, first assess risk as it pertains to your business model. Next, consider the different functional pieces that make up that business model.

SECURITY, OR LACK THEREOF, THROUGH COMPLIANCE

In our experience, we have never gone into a company where there has been no security whatsoever. The security that exists is typically driven not through business value but through compliance—in other words, risk avoidance from known penalties.

Simply put, there is a standards requirement of some kind—whether from the government as with HIPPA, SOX or PCI, or from other organizations—that is driving the need for security. The general assessment is the answer to the question, "Am I compliant, or not, to the standard?" On the surface, it seems to be why a company can say it has addressed threats and risks. The reality, though, is that building security to align with compliance standards makes the world a safer place only for those who put the standard out there in the first place. Compliance to these standards cannot be ignored, but they should not be used as a replacement to a real security strategy tailored to your company's own needs.

This approach of compliance-driven security results in "whack-a-product." This is the phenomenon of a security person focusing on the problem in front of them and a deadline for compliance. He or she quickly scrambles to buy some kind of software or service, slaps it on top of the problem, and then proceeds to react to the next emergency or deadline.

This often breeds a putting-out-fires kind of behavior. It comes not necessarily from blatant ignorance but from the fact that there are a lot of non-things in place that have no relevance to an actual security situation. In the chapters ahead, we discuss more of these that your company might be committing. Examples range from password procedures that get in the way to laptop sign-out procedures that are more security theater than security.

It's not a 100 percent win one way or the other. You may find a very mature company with great processes and procedures in place. They're very forward-thinking with security, but they're still going to have surprises.

We find that the companies that are a little bit insane in their thinking around security are the ones that I call the compliance-driven decision makers. Their concern might be, "Where am I going to get audited or lose money?", and that is how they identify risk. But they don't get robust with the list of things that can actually hurt them. For many companies, it's just lip service to brand damage.

The intangibles are very hard to put a dollar amount on. So if we had to go in front of a CFO and say, "You need to spend a million dollars to either (A) prevent brand damage or (B) prevent a $7 million fine," they are going to pay the million dollars to protect themselves from the $7 million fine because they can understand that on a spreadsheet.

So how can security be more effective? Any company's cyber-security can certainly be more effective, but it remains hard to get corporations behind it because of the intangible risks. This impacts funding allocation for security managers.

If I'm the CFO and I have multiple projects that I have to approve from a minimum amount of budget money, I'm going to allocate toward what increases profit or drives revenue. Security is not seen as a profit center.

VIEW OF SECURITY AS COST CENTER

Instead, security is frequently viewed as a cost center. Even if I am a CFO who is passionate about cybersecurity and security in general, it's still incredibly difficult to see that the money I spend is actually making a difference.

We assume that when you spend on security and you don't see problems, the money is working as intended. However, this can be hard to quantify to someone who does not see the threats on a daily basis. It is similar to Homeland Security saying, "The reason you haven't seen any attacks is because our methods are working." This can be difficult for the public to understand, when all it knows is that the lines are long at airports because of it.

And so it is with cybersecurity and your company's C-level executives.

From another perspective, when we spend money on marketing, we have no idea why it's working or not working. We might buy some newspaper ads and radio ads. We might also have some fun publicity events with giveaways and celebrities. For all three things combined, maybe we've spent in total $100,000 on marketing. If we see people coming in after that, we know we've had some degree of success.

Yet we might not have controllable metrics on which of those three efforts worked best or which was the most cost effective. We don't have anything proactive inside of the process letting us know which ads and which marketing channels are working.

If we do not do it in a strategic way, we are prisoner to what seems an unprovable process. Our company will always have to spend $100,000 for that same result because we do not know exactly what it is that is working.

The same thing is true with cybersecurity. We spend all this money, but we do not know if it is really making us secure. We do not know what's really important or what is simply a procedural legacy from a previous security manager. What we need is an overarching strategy and a way to update that strategy. What we need is a method, one where we can go back and say, "Is what we're doing today still necessary and still effective?"

To us, the discussion should be on spending time developing a strategy and monitoring how your strategy is working going forward. What some companies do very well is build a road map, execute the road map, and get to the end of the road map. Then, they high-five everybody as if it's mission accomplished.

What we do not see a whole lot of is measuring the impact of various procedures and plans. Yes, it can be hard to do, but it's worth it. Still, many companies operate with that old view, "No news is good news."

METRICS ADD VALUE TO MONITORING

Now, in thinking about how to combat this for your CEO and CFO, we would edit that statement slightly. We would say, "No news is good news, as long as it's backed up by metrics."

Put in a way that someone might be able to understand based on their home computer software, some antiviral programs have a pop-up window that tells you when it has blocked a potential viral attack. Now, that's all well and good, but the problem is that it may only be blocking 20 percent of the risks on your machine. Yes, it certainly is great when the system tells you that it blocks the one thing it knew how to. This makes you assume you are okay. Yet because it did not know how to identify seven other things that just happened, you might certainly not be.

This is how we become complacent in security, because we might not be asking the right questions, or we might be misinterpreting results.

That's the good thing about the frameworks and methodologies we discuss in this book because the proper systems force a nonemotional approach to cybersecurity.

Our ideas throughout this book will help you systemize your business processes around cybersecurity in such a way that you don't have to depend on gut feelings. You don't have to depend on what vendors are telling you. It is not a silver bullet, but it does help you make better decisions.

WHITE HOUSE INITIATIVES

We are beginning to see these principles being put in place by companies and other organizations. There has been a recent renaissance at the top levels in how companies look at security risks. We have seen this, for example, with the National Institute of Standards and Technology and the White House's cybersecurity recommendations, along with policies implemented by Duke Energy and Target.

Unfortunately, in the case of Target, this came after a major attack. Still, we are beginning to see large companies and governments taking the lead, and this helps trickle these ideas down to smaller companies.

In 2013, the White House decided Congress was taking too long to look at cybersecurity issues. It issued an executive order around the cybersecurity of critical national infrastructure.

The idea was to focus on things like the power grid, utilities, and water, along with other things that constitute critical national infrastructure. That became a looser descriptive term, and now more things are included in what is considered critical national infrastructure.

The economy in general is considered something that should be protected. Still, the White House and Congress chose not to try to put laws into effect and then have to enforce those laws. These became recommendations and guidelines.

What they told companies, and I'm paraphrasing here, was, "We're going to put the onus on you. If you are following a list of particular recommendations, you must get your vendors to toe the line."

The renaissance was then fueled through this process. Large enterprises were saying to smaller vendors that to work with them, they must improve their cybersecurity maturity level.

The good news is that this is not something new. In the analog world, this is exactly what companies do when dealing with a vendor that may damage property on-site. They make sure the vendor has insurance: if you don't have $15 million of liability coverage or whatever the figure, you can't come on-site to our facilities.

The cybersecurity initiatives were therefore expansions of current functioning business tools applied to vendors to make for continued improvements. The great thing is, companies that are progressive with cybersecurity are doing it in such a way that it lines up with the overall business objectives of their core enterprise.

They're not doing it just to be a pain in the neck to vendors. They are doing it because they're trying to have a successful business. To do that, they must have safe and successful partners and vendors with which to work.

For those of us in the IT security world, it is a really fascinating time to see this happening. Still, in our opinion, it is not happening enough. A lot of corporations have not been exposed to this concept in such a way that they are ready to take action on it.

We believe a lot of the smart IT people are up to speed on it, but it's the other side of the hall, the business line, that needs more education. They need to see a track record of success in other companies before they'll be ready to join this renaissance.

TRUE THREATS ARE HIDDEN IN THE NOISE

One of the lessons learned from Target's security breach was an ongoing issue with the FireEye cybersecurity tool they were using. The company was likely inundated with trivial true-positives—thousands and thousands of incident notifications. The true threats were hidden in the noise.

They just didn't have the proper incident response procedures in place. They likely didn't have the right resources—enough boots on the ground—to deal with what the tool was telling their security team in Minneapolis. The lesson in this case is that the data might be there, but you need the resources and people to be able to examine and interpret it properly. Read the Bloomberg article "Missed Alarms and 40 Million Stolen Credit Card Numbers: How Target Blew It" for a deeper dive.

If Target had taken the right approach, they would have detected the December 2013 breach, when their customers' credit card information stored in their systems was stolen, before it got out of hand.

That leads us to a question to ask yourself: Do you know if you have the correct processes and procedures in place to handle an emergency? Target's experience is a case where they had a bad situation and decided to slap a tool on it, but they didn't really have the bigger process to examine the resulting data.

If Target had been able to understand the possible threats coming their way and how the situation would present itself, they would more likely have had the technology to handle it. This is a case where a technology solution in a successful security implantation can protect you, but you must analyze business processes and possible risks so that you can build cybersecurity policies, processes, and procedures around it.

Let's move beyond Target and take a hypothetical company. A company has a system in place that keeps them very secure 99 percent of the time. That's great. But we want to focus on that 1 percent of the time when a bad actor comes in and does something totally off the charts, different from the other 99 percent of the time. Will you have the processes and procedures and the right human beings in place who will know how to react?

The big challenge is, how do you get ready for that 1 percent? And, when talking to the CFO, how do you justify the cost, and should you justify the cost? How do you mitigate the risks? The best thing you can do is gather as much information as possible. Understand. Know thyself. That helps you set up controls so that if the off-the-chart bad thing happens, you can make sure that your maximum risk is manageable.

It's not a matter of *if* it's going to happen. It's going to happen to everyone. You need to have the response planned.

In conversations with CFOs, one topic that might come up is cost-benefit analysis. Will we have to spend 99 percent of the budget for those 1 percent of issues? Small and medium-size companies might think they need to look at this differently from large businesses, or they might want to use large companies as models.

SECURITY IS A BUSINESS DECISION

Many people forget that security is a business decision. Simply put, you don't implement security if there's no business reason. This oversight has created many false assumptions inside of people's heads within the small and midsize business world.

We can't tell you how many times we hear, "Good thing I'm small enough that they don't care about me. They're only going after the big guys." People who say this don't understand the anatomy of a virus or an automated attack. Those types of threats don't distinguish by size.

It's about leveraging automation.

An analogy to help you and your higher-ups understand is a thief browsing through a parking lot in front of a mall. He goes to every single car, testing each handle, not targeting any one in particular. When he finds one unlocked, then he proceeds to steal or destroy whatever is inside. That's how many of these viral threats are. They test each system, not knowing what it is or who owns it, until they find one that is breachable.

What the small companies might still be saying to themselves is "Hey, I'm in this crowd of cars, and they're not going to come and find me because they're going to go find somebody else. They're not going to target me." The way that computer hacking scams work is that instead of having one thief, you have thousands of thieves.

The Home Depot payment system breach is a perfect example. Home Depot is a large company, but they weren't specifically targeted. The hackers were able to gain access to their network using stolen login credentials (keys, if you will) of a third-party vendor. The credentials happened to be valid, which allowed the hackers to gain initial entry into the network and find other vulnerable systems, allowing them to focus on attacking the payment system. The size of Home Depot made it a newsworthy event.[1]

The point, though, is that if it can happen to Home Depot, a large company you would expect to have great procedures in place, it can happen—and is happening right now—to small and midsize companies.

If you're heading cybersecurity at a midsize company and reading this book, you might be saying to yourself, "We've got a firewall and a router. We've got all our guys using some kind of encrypted Wi-Fi. We've got antivirus and some backup." Well that's fantastic. You might be safe, and you might not be.

The reality is, you have no idea if you're under attack or if you've already been breached, because you don't have detection tools. You don't even have detection processes and procedures, whereas the big guys like Home Depot, Target, and the state of South Carolina (which had Social Security numbers stolen) do have detection software in

---

1 Kumar, Devika Krishna. 2014. "Home Depot says about 53 million email addresses stolen in breach." *Reuters*, November 7. http://www.reuters.com/article/2014/11/07/us-home-depot-dataprotection-idUSKBN0IQ2L120141107

place. They have detection processes and procedures. They have a way to respond to the fact that they are being attacked.

The most terrifying thing for a midsize company would be to actually find out they're being attacked and having no idea what to do to fix it.

Of course, some small and medium companies might say to themselves that they don't really need to protect themselves. Right now, they might say, "What is the impact?" Most do not keep sensitive data that tends to be sold. When they do get a breach, typically the hackers are like "Ой, мужчина, мы получили в этих ребят? Там нет ничего хорошего здесь," a.k.a., "Aw, man, we got into these guys? There's nothing good here."

The real risk comes into play when these midsize companies attach to a larger enterprise that actually has something worth stealing. So the big risk for small and midsize companies is brand damage and the inability to get new business.

For many companies, this situation is not top-of-mind right now, because these events have not been in the news enough to be seen as a real problem. We do not have a lot of case studies that say Company XYZ failed to get this RFP or failed to get approved to work with this behemoth company because they didn't meet a minimum of cybersecurity standards. But you're fooling yourself if you do not think it's happening.

DISCONNECTION IN PROTECTION BELIEFS AND REALITY

Still, there is a wide division among companies when considering who among them has all the necessary procedures in place and who doesn't. A similar disconnect exists within companies between the cybersecurity staff people such as yourselves and the management teams.

A secure study by the Ponemon Institute states, "77 percent ... reported that their organizations experienced data breaches. All respondents noted they've had their data attacked in the last year, and 76 percent thought reducing potential security flaws within business-critical applications is the most important aspect of a data-protection program."[2] These statistics exemplify the strong disconnect between what the IT people know and the assumptions the C-level is operating under.

We have found that this comes from a variety of different factors. It's not just a matter of the poor social skills of an IT nerd. It's also a question of whether the organization is positioned to allow communication to flow up.

Part of the issue here, we've noticed, is that the IT nerds—the uber nerds as some call them—talk about *threats*, while the senior people in the company talk about *risks*. A company may have a good risk management program where risk mapping and prioritization is done.

We find that the IT people talk about security in a certain way among themselves, but it's really not tied to the company's overall operational framework in discussions. What this means is that connections aren't necessarily made when the IT people talk about how we need to do "A, B, and C." Since the IT folks make their recommendations in terms of threats and not risks, the executive does not

---

2 Ponemon Institute. 2010. "Business Case for Data Protection: A Study of CEOs and Other C-level Executives in the UK." IBM Software. http://www.findwhitepapers.com/content9704

make the connection to the risk that these actions are going to help mitigate. So tying threat to risk is critical.

At one company we worked with, the risk was called "loss of critical information." Yet when we went down and talked to the IT guys, they'd be talking about PII, IP, and HIPPA. This complex alphabet soup of terminology is a totally different language from that of upper management.

IT people must do better about working to align their bosses with security concerns. The technique we were taught is that if you're an IT professional, you have to talk to the other lines of business within the company. You have to understand what the other divisions are trying to produce and what they are trying to accomplish. This practice is called IT alignment, and there are a number of techniques for this that we won't elaborate on here.

If you're not proactive in talking with marketing, sales, and various research and development organizations and working to understand their goals, then they're really not going to want to talk to you. There simply won't be a lot of communication.

Often we find that IT folks handle things in the wrong way. For instance, they might be approached about a program someone wants to download off the Internet to handle an issue. IT might immediately say, "No, you can't do that, because policy says XYZ."

A better way is for IT to ask, "What are you trying to accomplish?" Once the employee coming to you for advice answers that question, a better response is "Okay, this policy we currently have in place to protect our systems is going to get in your way. Let's find a way to do what you want but in a way that doesn't violate this policy." Or, better yet, you might move further ahead and tell yourself, "Let's validate that this policy is still relevant to keep."

PROACTIVE IT DEPARTMENT COMMUNICATION

A good, smart IT person is proactive within his or her company's business functions, working as a problem solver, not a roadblock. That's very difficult because it takes a lot of different skills to have those kinds of conversations.

Cybersecurity people must try to see what the company is trying to achieve. When a CEO of a large company enacts mission and vision statements, that really gets the management and the senior directors fired up. That's totally MBA 101. For the rest of the human race—those without an MBA—understanding where a company or large organization is trying to go is very difficult.

So it's a two-way street here. It requires IT people to live in the business side, but it also requires the business side to be able to communicate expectations in such a way that IT people can work with them.

That's where our framework comes in. It creates the space for a shared language and a shared methodology, allowing these kinds of conversations to happen.

THE WHACK-A-MOLE PROBLEM OF SECURITY ISSUES

It becomes very difficult for companies to properly strategize while dealing with security issues one by one as they arise. It's like a whack-a-mole game. You don't know where they will come up, and you have to just hit back. It's important for companies to realize that as we address the immediate pain of problems as they arise, we're too focused on the issue at hand, and we don't have bandwidth to strategize. This allows us to get complacent with the status quo.

On top of this, many companies still maintain a view that "resistance is futile" with security problems, keeping investment on the issue to a minimum. I often hear, "No matter how much I spend, if somebody wants to get in, they're going to get in." That is the common wisdom. So when you're looking at cybersecurity from the business point of view, your management team is asking how much they should spend on something that can't be prevented anyway. That is the first point of resistance that we always have to confront.

We call that the sucker's choice. You're only giving yourself two possibilities: you're keeping attackers out all the time, or they're in all the time. You have to move to a way of understanding how to reach the correct level of risk mitigation. How do you make it so that if somebody does get in, you can detect and stop them or take some kind of action?

Basically, when you hear a statement that hackers will get in anyway, so what is the point, that's a victim mentality. Good cybersecurity methodology and good security methodology in general give you many other options, so you no longer have to say, "Hey, I'm a victim."

We must use cybersecurity as a platform for empowering organizations to move from victim to hero. This leads to the next step: a community working together for the sake of keeping their businesses and their broader industry as secure as possible.

Really, if you get down to it, cybersecurity folks are just rock stars. We'll just say it straight up. We're heroes. We are rock stars for the sales staff, who are expanding the size of the company. We are the rock stars for the customer service team answering questions for new and existing clients. We make sure it all runs and operates smoothly behind the scenes. Sometimes, this means being invisible. It always means we are working with all the divisions so that we are all rock stars together. The point is that we must work as a team. You can't be a rock star in the sales department if a security breach means people are afraid to make purchases with the company.

HOW DO SMART IT PEOPLE COMMUNICATE RISK?

There are many ways of tying things together to help those not in IT understand your—and therefore their own—security needs. At companies we have worked with, whenever we talk about cyber-security or requests for resources with a senior person, the very first thing we do is talk about how what we're doing ties directly to the overarching corporate strategy.

For example, the ambition of one company we work with is to grow sales. This is a natural desire for most companies. Regarding this ambition, they have stated that innovation is a key lever in achieving that growth strategy. So, in security meetings with higher-ups, we stress that security is related to protecting innovation, a key lever of our growth. That concept is how we start every conversation.

It is an easy thing for most of the people in the business line to understand. After all, their bonuses are based on hitting that growth target. So we're hoping that by talking about security in terms of business strategy first, everyone can see how it fits in.

> So it's not about a victim mentality, as we've seen in some companies. By discussing security as part of the overarching business plan and economic goals of the company, it's easy for everyone in the meeting room to understand.

In addition, we know that in any company, bad things can happen. This approach ensures you're in a position to do something about it rather than just sit there and get kicked.

This overarching business plan and protecting the company's growth targets go back to the example we had where a lack of security allowed a television network's show plans to leak. That's an attack on the company's advertising revenue. For other companies, it might be a secret formula not yet patented or the chemical composition of a new drug under development. It might be details about a buyout of another company you're keeping under wraps.

Companies that understand this are usually those that have something naturally easy to lose via a security breach. When intellectual capital is stolen, the intention is to take that intellectual capital and turn it into money.

Or cyberattacks can skip all that by just going in and getting the money directly. Financial institutions understand that there are people out there who will try to take their money. It's very real, very tangible.

So, in our opinion, within the private sector industries, financial institutions are the leaders in cybersecurity. They're on it. They understand it. And they've spent a lot of money on it, too.

Intellectual property companies also understand it because it's their competitive advantage. When you have grown a business from nothing to a multibillion-dollar firm, your trademarks, patents, and secrets—all your how-to knowledge—are what drive the value within the company. If those were to get out, those advantages would go away, and what was a prosperous, healthy business that provided jobs and security for thousands of people becomes at risk.

Pharmaceutical companies also understand, considering the billions they spend on research and development.

CYBERSECURITY IN THE
MEDICAL FIELD

Interestingly enough, hospitals have not taken the same view as pharmaceutical companies on cybersecurity—even if we might lump both together in our minds as health-care companies. A hospital is concerned with human care, the physical body that is damaged in some way. Hospitals want to repair that body and get it out the door in a way that is more positive than when it came in. In some ways, that is akin to a retail company. We might think very few cybersecurity issues are in the middle of that mission, right?

However, the damage comes in the tertiary factors around that experience, primarily around the personal data of the patient. Since they are not primary factors in the success of the hospital's mission, cybersecurity concerns often take a backseat. A hospital manager instead thinks, do I invest in this new piece of machinery that can do dialysis and help children, or do I spend on cybersecurity detection and awareness software?

This is changing as the digital age becomes more prevalent inside hospitals and as hospitals gather more information about their patients. Still, there are few controls, and an IT security person inside a hospital does not have much power to enact change without the executives prioritizing it in the right way.

When we look at companies that are successful with cybersecurity, we find that their executives have a real business need to prioritize it. They recognize that cybersecurity is also where their competitive advantage can be in relation to other companies.

TECHNOLOGY IS OUTPACING CYBERSECURITY

Technology is outpacing the ability to secure it. A kid with a Dell laptop and some easily available hacking tools can access a lot of your information.

That's a very bad thing, and at the same time it's a wonderful thing because the causes of that reality are innovation and new products. All of these new ways of doing things also affect human behavior—for example, the iPhone that automatically backs up your photos so that if you lose the phone you can get those pictures back.

I have my six-year-old daughter's entire life photographed and videotaped on my iPhone. Losing all of those precious moments would be awful, so I've transferred the data. And the fact that it's backed up is great news.

However, often user experience outpaces the people who are trying to secure the data. Security can be a slower-moving beast than business innovation. There will always be a percentage of technology outpacing its security.

Security in the cloud is one example, as celebrities like Jennifer Lawrence and others have discovered through the theft of their iCloud credentials. But for the practical purposes of a company, it's about capital, storage, hosting, and similar functions. Different companies do these kinds of backups and security procedures at different levels.

Another pertinent example is the smart meter technology that transmits data from one's home or office so that it can be readily scanned by energy companies.

One benefit of these for home users is potential understanding of optimum energy usage for environmental reasons. In reality, however, the real reason those meter readers exist is so that power companies know how much power to produce. If a company can tell in real time that current power production needs are ten units, for example, and they are producing eleven, they know they are wasting resources and money. Understanding this is also key to trending an analysis of what they have done over the last twenty years to project future energy usage.

It's fantastic technology for sure, but with the Internet of Things, companies are putting devices in people's homes that are going back up the copper wiring into hubs. Now, there's going to be some kid who will be able to plug into your home network.

I personally run my home network over my electrical cables inside my house along with some Wi-Fi. Being able to bridge the gap between the electric smart grid and my house will allow that kid, or anyone else smart enough, access to multiple homes throughout the neighborhood.

When the power companies got together to look at this problem, they basically said it wasn't a big enough issue for them to be concerned about. That might be fair, considering the chances that this will happen on any given system. Other potential data intrusions might be much more pressing. Still, a business on that system with innovations worth stealing can lose all of its investment by not properly examining security.

> You might feel your company's system is secure, but what about the networks it's connected to? This is what we are working to get you to think about.

SECURITY GLITCHES CAN DESTROY A COMPANY

An example we like to relate involves the plans of the CMO of a large company. They determine that a smartphone application is what they need to grab market share. They spend two years and $16 million creating this amazing smartphone app that does all this exciting stuff, and best of all, makes the retail experience better and faster.

Then three weeks after release, the app is compromised and hacked. All of the customer data gathered through the amazing launch gets stolen. Now the application is no longer trusted, and this innovation, which was supposed to bring bountiful wealth and opportunity, is a giant eyesore. And it destroys the company.

For us, the lesson here is in this: How can we take a business's need to grow, innovate, and produce new value and bring it into a system that allows them to do just that—but in such a way that the smart people handling the security can ensure that the value the company is creating is retained beyond an attack?

This is not hypothetical. Of the one hundred top-selling Android and iPhone apps, more than three out of four of them, or 78 percent, have been hacked. A study on the Arxan website, "State of Security in the App Economy," shows that 92 percent of the paid iPhone apps and 100 percent of the paid Android apps have been hacked.[3]

In our cars, auto companies have been installing computers for years now. White-hat hack guys have demonstrated how easy it is to get into vehicle IT systems. In our bodies, one great recent innovation for pacemakers—Wi-Fi connection—allows us to modify the device without going back into a person's chest through risky surgery. But of course this Wi-Fi connection creates a new risk as part of the Internet of Things. We shudder to mention this because we wonder who in their right mind would attach malicious software to pacemaker Wi-Fi networks, causing them to malfunction and throw recipients into a heart attack. Think about how many national leaders have pacemakers.

This was in the news when former Vice President Dick Cheney had his put in.

One of our favorite phrases when explaining these principles to clients is that security is like sex in a marriage. It's an indicator of how the marriage is doing. If you have a bad sex life, and sex is a topic you

---

3 Arxan Technologies. "State of Security in the App Economy." Accessed on Sept. 2, 2015. https://www.arxan.com/resources/state-of-security-in-the-app-economy-info-graphic/

can't talk about, chances are there are other things in the marriage that are breaking down trust and the ability to be intimate.

If you have bad security in your company, chances are people aren't talking to each other. Communication is bad. The trust isn't there.

But if you have a mature security environment, one that adapts to changes, then what you've got is great communication. You've got the ability to be self-aware and the assurance that it's okay to be wrong at times. You don't point fingers. Instead, you learn from mistakes, and you have a nurturing relationship inside the company.

We think it is completely accurate to say that if you find a large company or midsize company's willingness to talk about and address security concerns at a mature level, you are in a great space to work.

INDUSTRIES THIS BOOK WILL HELP

In this book we draw examples from several industries: power, health, manufacturing, retail, finance, education, engineering, federal government, and state government.

Even if your company does not exactly fit into these various types, many of the examples will be of help to you. We also give real-life examples of companies that have been attacked, how they responded, and what lessons you can draw for your own company. There are lots of problems that will come your way, but that does not mean they cannot be fixed and discussed with your C-suite management.

And that is how we aim to make this book one of the most useful tools in your arsenal.

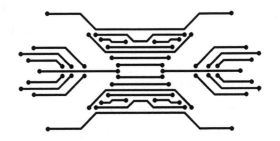

CHAPTER 2

LEARNING FROM INDUSTRY EXAMPLES AND INTRODUCING FRAMEWORKS

I n the previous chapter, we tell you about all the various industries this book examines: power, health, manufacturing, retail, finance, education, engineering, federal government, and state government. Although there's a commonality among how we go about it, the actual execution takes a different form for each of these.

So we have the utility industry with power, water, gas, and so on. We've got health care, including insurance companies and medical providers such as hospitals, doctors, and everything involved in that delivery. We have manufacturing, retail, finance, education, engineering, and state and federal government. The list goes on and on and on.

The key point, though, is that even if your business does not exactly fit into the categories, there are commonalities among all these industries with your own when it comes to making security a priority.

If you look at the financial industry, their issues are at the high end of the due diligence component of the security model and framework. Power is also at that level of attention. The good news is that the lessons learned from these industries can be applied in manufacturing and government.

Cybersecurity is a spiderweb of connectivity, and in order to have a net that will catch the bad guys and keep us safe, you will have to depend on interactions with every point of this web.

Focusing only on your own industry or area is not enough. We feel that the topic of peer networks—getting out there and getting input from other people—is important enough to warrant its own chapter, chapter 3, where we discuss them in detail. The idea of peer groups is also woven throughout this book.

Your peer groups are an extension of your security framework, a model system that allows you to have a conversation with people who might not be in your industry but who still speak the same language of cybersecurity.

WATCHING CYBERSECURITY GROW

Developing cybersecurity and how to address risk is an extremely interesting topic to us, especially since we've watched the field grow over the long period of time we've been working within it.

In the beginning, cybersecurity was primarily a vendor-driven experience, where salespeople would come in and educate customers on why they should be afraid. Now what we see happening is CFOs and CIOs and directors of security taking responsibility for redefining risk.

The old strategy of the salesperson coming in and scaring everybody doesn't seem to work as well as it once did. The folks higher up in a company making the business decisions are beginning to understand cybersecurity risk as it pertains to business value.

Indeed, there are a blinding number of vendor solutions. We could spend forty hours a week just talking to all the vendors coming to us with scary stories and attached solutions.

> With such a sea of solutions, if you don't have a good focus on what your true risks are, you'll flounder and end up signing contracts for things that sound good but may not address the real risks you're facing.

What we see in the field is that it is almost as if the vendor selling process has become white noise—the same group of people coming in again and again, doing the same song and dance about cybersecurity needs (or at least what they believe are your needs).

FRAMEWORKS HELP GUIDE YOUR CYBERSECURITY STRATEGY

When a proactive company moves away from being educated by vendors on how to protect itself and starts creating frameworks and introducing standards into those frameworks, it is empowered to take ownership of its cybersecurity.

> However, this is where the question must be asked: "Am I doing this out of fear because a vendor is coming in and telling me of my risks, or am I owning it and going through the pains of figuring it out?"

We believe it's important for a company, or for a security staff, to be honest about how it is making security decisions. It does not matter where you are in this process, you just need to know where you are and decide where you want to be.

> That comes down to data points and analysis. You can't know yourself and can't identify where you are without information.

Frequently, decisions are made in a security world around what the security people know, even if that is not a complete picture. Self-awareness inside a company is very important. The good news about a framework is that it allows everyone to start from the same place.

It's okay to be a beginner when you enter into the world of designing a framework. What we find is that many in IT also feel pressure to always have the answer when speaking to other lines of the business, be it C-level or human resources. In contrast, when you look at a framework, you're saying that none of us has the right answer. That's a huge thing. We're only going to be able to be about 10 percent accurate at this time. Let's all be beginners together and make ourselves better in the process.

FRAMEWORKS AND PEER GROUPS

Frameworks break down barriers. They allow for conversations that wouldn't have happened otherwise.

As an example, I was sitting in a boardroom, and we were talking to twenty CIOs about the cybersecurity framework. On my left, I had some folks from energy, and on my right, I had some folks from health care.

The guy from health care had about forty peers in other hospital systems that he could talk to about cybersecurity. Now, because he was in the hospital system, no one had money to spend, but at least they were talking to each other.

His primary resources for the strategies and testing decisions he was making were not the people inside his company; his primary resources were other people tackling the same problems in other companies. They were able to share lessons in security from forty different hospital systems across the United States.

That is not something that happens very often. Still, they were missing the boat on one thing: they were only talking to other hospital systems.

CROSS-DIVISION COMMUNICATION

My goal and my vision would be "Hey, let's get these folks talking to manufacturing. Let's get these folks talking to finance. Let's get them talking to as many other industries as possible so that they get many different perspectives on security."

When a threat is in the world and you've got a bad hacker trying to attack you, that hacker is going to come at you in many different ways. That's when those many different lessons are invaluable.

I'm sure if we went to Ukraine and started interviewing people, they would not have "I hack health care" or "I hack finance" on their business cards. They hack everyone, and they apply what they've learned from all other industries when they attack a target.

And, if the bad guys have their peer groups, we good guys had better make sure we have ours.

Sometimes peer groups are informal, ad hoc groups. Sometimes they happen spontaneously at conferences. Peer groups are about networking and making personal connections, and exploring common challenges.

On a cautionary note, some international groups have evolved into platforms where vendors can engage with customers or security vendors can engage with security practitioners and sell them services. You have to avoid those pitfalls.

One peer group that we enjoy is the International Security Managers Association. It has a great online forum, where a chief security officer can say, for example, "Hey, how are you guys dealing with the hostage situation in Paris? Have you restricted travel?" or, "What's a good cybersecurity company vendor in Nigeria that you guys would trust?" Discuss real, practical information that evolves for current threats.

These peer networks are important because through them, you can get advice detailing who picked certain vendors and why. In one forum survey, approximately 65 percent of participants indicated that they picked certain vendors because "I know somebody who has done business with this vendor before and recommended them."

In security, it's all about trust. It is very hard to quantify or qualify that trust and how we assess a new company, but that being said, having somebody whom we trust and who trusts us—that's the key.

The advice and guidance in cybersecurity can help with physical security as well—they both go hand in hand. For example, we needed a good West Coast resource to help with executive protection for our senior leadership. We didn't have a relationship with someone out there who could provide professional bodyguard type service, so we contacted a security colleague at a large tech company in Silicon Valley. We asked, "Hey, who do you guys use for executive protection?" Tom also spoke with the chief security officer at a large Seattle-based software giant and asked, "Who do you guys use?" Based on their recommendation, we signed an agreement with the company they used.

A framework allows you to have a formal process for having a vendor self-assess. You can then audit that company's self-assessment. This gives you something objective from which to make a decision.

THE FIVE COMPONENTS OF THE NIST CYBERSECURITY FRAMEWORK

In the National Institute of Standards and Technology's Cybersecurity Framework, there are five primary categories: Identify, Protect, Detect, Respond, and Recover. They go like this:

1. Identify: What do you own (information, intellectual property, infrastructure...)?

2. Protect: How do you protect assets from threats?

3. Detect: How do you detect attacks?

4. Respond: How do you respond?

5. Recover: How do you repair and bounce back?

We go into greater detail on each of these points in its own chapter.

I can go into a doctor's office for a particular something wrong with me. The doctor might begin rattling off a lot of medical terminology. My wife, for example, is a pediatric nurse, and she tries to convince me of medical issues using fact.

She uses a lot of industry standard terms and concepts, like this or that new drug, your cholesterol's too high, and so on. She tells me I should do this, that, or another thing for my health concerns. I have to say that I absolutely lose the impetus to try to change because I just get glazed eyes.

There's nothing wrong with the education she's giving me. She's giving me facts the same way that doctors do. The key, however, is the way in which that education is given—as facts indiscriminately coming my way. I am not equipped with a pre-med, four-year degree allowing me to absorb this impromptu education.

We stress this point because while education is important, you must know your audience and educate them in the right way. When my doctor's talking about my high cholesterol and running through the available medicines, I look at him and say, "I don't know all this. I don't even want to know all this. You're the subject matter expert—you tell me what to do." At this point, I am passive in my own treatment.

That seems easy, and it is how many people approach their own health care, but it is not the right answer, in our opinion. The right answer is for the doctor to speak to us in language we can understand so that we can have a real conversation about my health. That is the direction we think cybersecurity needs to go.

I will do another analogy. I recently started the training and fitness program CrossFit. Part of the CrossFit mentality is the physical exercise, along with a diet to complement it, among other components.

They have a framework for physical fitness and total health. There are dangers: if you go too fast or have the wrong form, you might get hurt; if you don't do the diet correctly, you won't get the results you want. But they break all of these issues down in a way that resonates with me.

That is the kind of thing we want the education of security to be for businesses: if you do these things, here are the results—presented in a way that you can understand.

SOFTWARE TOOLS TO EVALUATE YOUR CYBERSECURITY MATURITY

It is for these reasons that we in the security industry have developed evaluative software tools—tools that allow you to look at these NIST security pillars, assess where you are as a company, build a target for where you want to be, and help provide you with a road map for success to reach that target.

The point of software in technology in general is to modify human behavior. When you find a desirable human behavior, you can use technology as a multiplier effect of that human behavior. Let's use Facebook as an example. We want to talk to people and stay in touch with people who are friends. But in order for us to send pictures and share things, we can use email, write letters, or visit them face-to-face. Facebook allows you to share among a variety of people, with just a few simple clicks.

There are costs to that as well. Sitting in front of someone resonates differently than communicating via a Facebook post. But when you're very focused on what you are trying to deliver, software is a great way of replicating a human behavior that you want to replicate.

We had an experience watching a large utility company talk to a security vendor. The utility company said, "We need to look at cybersecurity more seriously. This is how we're doing it. We want you to come back in six weeks and tell us what you're going to do."

After examining things, the vendor said, "We appreciate you bringing this to our attention. Here are the changes we're going to make," and they made the changes. But that vendor worked with multiple utilities and multiple people, and the amazing thing was the ripple effect that happened.

This one utility company taking a step forward in its security affected the entire power grid. We thought, "Whew. How did they do that?" They used the NIST security model. They used those five points we discussed earlier.

But there are precious few human beings who not only understand the NIST security model or a framework like it but are also able to have a human conversation with folks. So the challenge for us is how can we replicate this conversation as many times as possible?

We have our own software solution for this, but there are others. For example, there are GRCs, standing for governance, risk, and compliance. In a GRC, you have a conversation and everything gets stored in the software. They are very complicated and cumbersome, and it really takes an expert to use them.

MAKING IT SIMPLE

We consider applying the pregnancy test model to cybersecurity. Once, for a woman to discover she was pregnant, she had to take a blood test, a complex process that was not all that private. Now, she can go to a corner drugstore and choose from an array of products to find out if she is pregnant privately, using the device at home.

Let's look at this in comparison. We have a complex system of testing blood to find out what enzymes, hormones, and whatever else is going on to see whether the female body is acting differently, versus an easy at-home test. Taking this example for cybersecurity, we have a very complex security conversation that needs to happen. Providing a simple and effective tool that allows that conversation to happen in a less threatening way and allows the person who needs the discovery to have more control is a good thing.

That's the whole purpose here. We are not suggesting that you need a software product. However, there are a lot of good people out there making good tools that you should consider, and that can really assist in making this conversation easier.

All of this allows you to understand where you currently are in the NIST Framework, along with where you need to be. But through it all, the key is to go only as far as you need to, keeping it in line with business value.

Once you know where you are and where you want to be, you can come up with a plan or a road map that'll take you from Point A to Point Success.

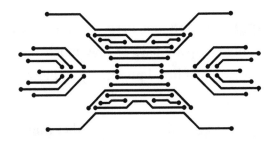

CHAPTER 3

DON'T GO IT ALONE—CREATING PEER GROUPS WITH OTHER EXECUTIVES

I am currently part of a business owners peer group. The catalyst for this detailed chapter on peer groups is that Tom and I have witnessed the great value in forming peer group among security folks.

In this chapter, we highlight the value of these peer groups and the need to create them for security professionals. This is perhaps also the most deeply psychological of our chapters, hitting at some of the emotions you might feel as you try to solve your company's ongoing security issues.

I am a business owner. So far in my lifetime, I've had fourteen businesses. I'm launching my fifteenth right now. I am frequently alienated from the rest of the human race because many people who have never been entrepreneurs do not share the experiences that I have.

An ordinary person does not have to worry about the twenty mortgages that my company pays or how much money I keep on hand for risk mitigation or how I protect my employees or how I deal with problems.

Often a person can get to the point where they think no one understands them—that no one can possibly relate to what they're going through—which is understandable, because everyone has individual experiences, whether a business owner, a race-car driver, a doctor, or whatever they might be. It doesn't matter. Everyone has experiences that are tailored to their human condition.

I joined an organization called Chief Executive Boards International, made up of about 150 small to midsize business owners who get together and sit in boards of around eight to ten folks. We have a moderator-led discussion, where each of us has the opportunity to bring certain topics and concerns to the table.

I remember the first time I was in there. I thought everyone was going to be talking about financial concerns or, "Oh, I have employee," and so and so forth. It turns out that it's much more complicated than that.

I would say that only 20 percent of our conversations have anything to do with business. They have everything else to do with experiencing life in a particular role.

An example is one gentleman whose wife was dying of cancer and how he approached that. He could have had that conversation with a lot of different people, but with this group of people, he knew we understood where part of his concerns were. We could speak his language.

Some members are having problems with their children. Some are having problems with key employees. What I learned is that I need peer groups not just for the business side but also for the life side, with folks who understand my concerns and what I'm talking about.

PEOPLE SKILLS

I looked at a lot of professional services organizations and peer groups in the security field. My frustration with these firms was that typically you have a security manager who has been promoted from a tech point of view.

These folks typically do not have what we would call people skills. However, quite often, when they have to deal with security problems, it's not the technology that's the issue, it's getting people to perform tasks necessary for the desired result. At the end of the day, they have all the tools they need, but their people just are not performing. What do they do?

That conversation is the most important conversation you can have, so that is the focus of this chapter. We understand that it is easy to feel helpless and alone, but the truth of the matter is that there are thousands of people going through the same thing. You just need to meet them.

It's very easy to deny that there's any problem at all because you feel alone. You'd rather ignore it than try to conquer this massive thing. Again, we must reiterate the fact that human behavior is typically the issue. When this behavior isn't managed correctly, it can create risks in your company's systems.

For example, a disgruntled security employee is the most risky person in your company. He or she might have access to ways to damage the financial security and integrity of your company.

SUPPORT AMONG PEERS WHO SPEAK AND INTERPRET YOUR LANGUAGE

Among the things that can be discussed in peer groups is the context of problem solving for people responsible for security. Sometimes, there is simply a need for members of the group to talk about articulating and getting the resources needed from senior management to do the job. It's hard at times to translate our uber-tech speak into business language.

Having a peer group allows us to find out from other peers how they were able to craft the message, make the business case, and get the resources they needed. That's a key way that peer groups can help: they allow you to find ways to articulate what you need to do and communicate within your company to get the resources you need.

For example, I just promoted a new president, and he is not prepared. But he's fantastic, and we love him at the company. There are many things he excels in, and he's a great operations guy. To help him with the things he does not yet know, one of his requirements now is to join a peer group.

We've tossed him in the deep end, and we know he is out of his depth. Without people there to help him learn to swim in those waters, he's in trouble.

The same is true with new security executives. They can handle the technology problems, but they've got to learn how to communicate that to others. People already think they're superhuman because of their technical skills, but it's getting people to understand their language that's important. People trust them because they're good at security, but it is really about the next step.

When we don't have a repeatable process and we don't have a repeatable system that we can measure and create policies and procedures around, typically what we do is fall back on superhuman effort—a hero coming in and fixing the problem when no one else knows what's going on. That is a fantastic way to start because at this point we don't know what we need to be doing. We require these superheroes.

At some point, though, heroes become a liability. They are not scalable. In order to be successful, we need to learn lessons from our superheroes and create processes and procedures that normal human beings can do and follow and audit and be held accountable to.

That's how we need to grow, and that can be a very difficult thing. We ask somebody, "How do you do what you do?" and basically they say, "I have no idea. I just get in there and win."

BUILDING FRAMEWORKS MAKES US ALL SUPERHUMAN

This superhero phenomenon is in every industry—it's not solely about cybersecurity—and it is a key risk that needs to be addressed. One way that you can help superheroes get their information across is by adopting a framework.

In some ways, this acts like a bridge, getting you to the next level. You have your superhero and you get things done, but when it's time to scale, you have a bridge. You take him or her and plug them into the framework model. The framework, because it's software, is scalable and repeatable.

In olden days, we had the apprenticeship model. We would have the superhero have an apprentice, and that person would be trained to eventually become a master. That model works very well if you remain the same size.

But when you have to give that superhero ten apprentices, things break down, and that's where scalability comes into play. Sometimes a systemized approach will mean you have to lower standards slightly as you expand, but you will still have desired results in the long run.

PEER GROUPS COST MONEY

Peer groups cost money, and people don't want to spend money. The only people who have a vested interest in a peer group are vendors, so often a vendor creates a peer group as a form of sponsorship and brings people in, then uses the group as market research.

That means the peer group is skewed. If I am an IBM vendor and I bring you in and there's a problem, I'm going to give you the IBM flavored solution.

That is a risk with vendor-led peer groups. It doesn't mean they're bad. It just means you need to be aware, since you're not going to hear about every possible solution to your problem.

A healthy fear of the challenges you face and how to react to them is necessary. However, in our opinion, this need for a call to action means it is important to be a part of a vendor-agnostic peer group. Typically what that means is that you're going to need to spend money—your own money—rather than let the vendor fund the whole thing.

Peer groups do not work unless they can function in an environment of trust, safety, and confidence. This means that we know and agree that what we say in front of these eight human beings or ten human beings does not leave the room, because there are trade secrets that need to be said to drive the point home. There are also personal things that need to be said.

For example, the team from BMW is not going to feel comfortable talking to you about security concerns if you're going to go and talk to folks over at Volvo.

FREE OPTIONS VERSUS PAYING FOR PEER GROUPS

There are also other types of peer groups. One is a self-led peer group, where a bunch of folks get together and talk. Another is a moderator-run peer group, which usually has a cost.

You can do a free version, but our experience has been that it is better to allot some cash and have a moderator who has been there and done that and can make sure that things stay on track. He or she might lead the group by saying, "You only have fifteen minutes to show your problem because we need to give you thirty minutes for questions and answers." That way, people in the group are held accountable. They stay on topic because they know people are putting real time and money into it.

With peer groups like this, you are basically paying somebody to be a strong voice and keep people on track. In a free group, there is a possibility of getting a few people who are very vocal and monopolize the time. If you don't have an authority in there, the group can become useless.

We do not think a moderator-run peer group is appropriate for everyone in a company trying to tackle issues. Still, a moderator-led peer group is appropriate for security because we're dealing with a very important issue, and we need somebody to hold everybody accountable and to keep track.

There is also a little bit of risk regarding liability and deferring that to somebody else when using moderators.

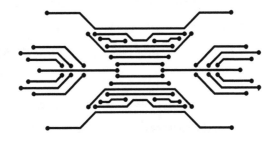

CHAPTER 4

FRAMEWORK PRINCIPLE 1: HOW DO YOU IDENTIFY WHAT YOU OWN?

I n the next several chapters, we are going to break down the principles of frameworks, as defined by the NIST.

From the NIST Cybersecurity Framework Document:

Identify. *Develop the organizational understanding to manage cybersecurity risk to systems, assets, data, and capabilities. The activities in the Identify function are foundational for effective use of the Framework. Understanding the business context, the resources that support critical functions, and the related cybersecurity risks enable an organization to focus and prioritize* *its efforts, consistent with its risk management strategy and business needs. Examples of outcome categories within this function include: asset management; business environment; governance; risk assessment; and risk management strategy.*

We must know what we own. We can't protect what we don't even know we own. We need to assess this in order to know where to begin and the scope of what we are looking to protect.

Essentially, this principle is about asset management. It's the "know thyself" side of the equation. Before we can do anything, we must know what we actually have.

Step one is to take inventory of what we own. This includes not just our IT security infrastructure but also information. By information, we mean intellectual property, client list, company credit cards that associates use, and personally identifiable information, such as employees' Social Security numbers and other such records.

How you answer the question "What do I have?" will depend on where you are coming from. IT people will look at physical assets like servers, laptops, network devices, firewalls, and any number of devices used to store or consume and make use of data. They will also look at the data itself—in the form of software the company is using and the data that software is producing and storing.

Let's list out a few things to consider: information assets, your networks, your computer hardware, your software applications, your network environment, and your end points. These are all assets.

GOVERNANCE

Do you have a governance structure in place to make decisions on how to classify data? Who makes decisions on what kind of firewalls you're going to put in place, for example?

Does your company have a process for identifying what assets it should be concerned about? We will give you an example. We tell people that compliance with standards is not the goal of security, but it's a great place to start. We can't get it all in the first try, but we can have a plan.

Yes, you have to do compliance because as an industry standard, that's a given. If you don't do it, you may not be able to sign contracts or do business. So while we sound as if we're being dismissive of standards because we believe they only scratch the surface, you must still take care of them. In a way, however, compliance is merely a superficial sign of being secure. Once you get the standards out of the way, you still must understand your business and its own specific security needs.

If you're going to protect your critical assets, you have to know which assets are genuinely critical to your business. As an example, how long can your CRM database be down without affecting revenue?

If you look at asset management, it's basically about building a list of business tools, systems, and information necessary for the business to succeed. These can be physical, such as facility and hardware. They can be software or data related, or the secret sauce itself—intellectual capital. Or they can be how we do what we do in our business processes. To us, those are assets even if they seem physically intangible, unlike a factory or a set of laptops.

It's always been very hard for us to prioritize assets. We think that's the role of the security executive—to go through and apply the right amount of pressure to the right assets so that this massive beast can be quantified.

The business environment is what helps you pick your asset management strategy. You know that certain lines of businesses are more important than others. For example, your R&D is very important for your strategic success, but it doesn't matter at all if you're having a tactical cash flow problem.

Being in tune with how your business operates—how it makes decisions and does what it needs to do—will help you prioritize inside the framework.

Remember, in this book we outline a framework of things to think about, but how you approach that is going to be based on your individual company and the people inside your company.

Governance to us is a very ethereal thing. We're certainly not comfortable with no governance at all, because governance is how you go about being compliant and how you establish what policies to adhere to. But, as we have said, there is something superficial about it. It seems to suggest you're secure, but that is not necessarily the case.

WHEN MANDATORY TRAINING GETS IN THE WAY

Regarding mandatory training, here's an example we are dealing with at a large manufacturing company we are working with. We have different online business unit functions, like human resources, legal, security, audit, finance, and others. All of these groups have "mandatory training" that they would like to deploy to the workforce.

Okay, there are twenty-two thousand employees, most of whom are blue-collar manufacturing people. Every minute they're not on the manufacturing line making tires, or whatever product, costs the company money. It hits our productivity levels.

Yet, for example, human resources says we must have mandatory discrimination training. As security manager, I say we must have information security training. The legal department says we need to administer ethics training. Each division is mandating to the entire workforce, "You have to take my mandatory training."

There's no overarching "governance" body that's signing off on what should be mandatory. Everyone individually is making these proclamations, and they are doing it without any kind of governance looking at the different trainings. Nobody is weighing which ones are really the most important or making decisions on how much training time each employee should have each year.

When we think of governance, this is one thing we think about. You need a high-level referee and business executive deciding what's going to be done and what's not going to be done. Otherwise the raccoons in your organization will just turn over all the garbage cans and mess everything up. At the same time, for governance to be successful, deciding what is important must have executive sponsorship.

The issue with the different divisions is important because there are so many people who have an opinion throughout a company. How do you align those opinions, and how do you align those objectives in such a way that we can actually accomplish something with them?

Let's be clear about what we mean by governance before you start thinking we need to have Congress involved. There are these things called IT governance and IT alignment. They are basically the big grandfather of a framework for various parts. IT alignment regards what a business is supposed to do and how technology aligns with that.

IT governance involves actually testing to see if that alignment is happening. When we're looking at governance, we're saying, especially around assets, that we should be going out there to know where every single laptop is and what every single BYOD or device that employees choose to use is doing, and where the intellectual capital is, and who has access to what. Governance is going in and testing and validating and reporting on how well we're accomplishing that mission.

RISK ASSESSMENT

A common theme throughout the framework is not what you should be doing. Instead, it is how you prove that you are doing what you should be doing.

As a company, if you're following the NIST Framework, someone can come in and say, "Prove to me you have controls in place and you're complying." You need to have a second level of control to show that you're doing all the things you say you're doing.

The next thing to consider is risk assessment. Risk assessment is near and dear to our hearts because it is a simple concept that is executed in a plethora of ways. It is basically saying, "We are going to do something new. We are going to introduce something into the company and its IT environment—we want to know, what is the impact?"

Now, on the surface, that statement seems very straightforward. When you put that task in front of somebody, however, that's where it gets complicated. What we find in the industry is that there are a lot of questions around risk assessment, and every company seems to do it its own way. There are some standards, but at the end of the day, the line of business tends to take a stand against risk assessment.

The important thing to think about in reading this book is that many of you are coming from various backgrounds within a company. Some of you are security professionals, completely in tune with much of what we cover in the book, and some of you are corporate people and business line people who want to understand how to work with security professionals.

The question then is, what is risk assessment, and why is it important? Risk assessment allows you to prioritize. You've only got so many dollars. You have a million things that you just inventoried.

Risk assessment allows you to focus and prioritize your dollars and security resources. We figure out what our vulnerable systems are, who is trying to steal our stuff, what it is exactly that people most want to steal, and where that stuff is. Then we go prioritize all of our systems based on the vulnerability and the business risks those systems represent.

Then with the resources we can obtain, we protect those systems the best we can. We are guessing that Google probably spends more money protecting their data centers than they do protecting the server that holds the lunch menu at Mountain View for the nineteen or however many employee cafes they have. They know what is more valuable to their business

The way security thinks about risk, we want to be involved at the beginning. We want to understand what you are trying to accomplish in the business line. We want to help you make good decisions on what you're supposed to be doing and what you're not supposed to be doing.

We want businesses to understand the actions they're about to take and the risks that are in there. That's the security way of thinking about risk. The business owner thinks about risk as dollars and cents. The security person looks at it with the mind-set of, "What is my total risk financially for doing something, and do my opportunities outweigh my risks?"

For a security person, all risk is bad. A business line person or a CEO thinks, "Give me the information I need to make an intelligent risk decision." A risk assessment is supposed to be a data point in a larger decision process.

TRIAGING RISK

In some cases as a business owner, you may decide based on the dollar amount to accept the risk instead of mitigating it. One way to think about this is triage, or rather pre-triage, since you're deciding ahead of time, before damage, what things are more mission critical than others. That is where you'll put your security dollars when you have a budget limit on what you can spend.

Risk assessment helps you decide ahead of time, before an issue strikes, what you can live with, what you can live without, and what is mission critical. You will prioritize spending and effort based on those decisions.

If we look at it in an almost medical way, what we're doing is assessing all the different things and providing the data points back to the physician so that the physician can decide what patient gets attention first.

With small businesses, which have far more limited resources and staff, this need to prioritize is more of an issue, and risk assessment is also often harder to deal with simply from the standpoint of time.

Most of what we have been describing is how a large business with a staff of experts goes about doing things. Practically speaking, for most small or midsize businesses, there usually has been no risk-assessment process in place. You do whatever you need to do to survive for that day. As a small business owner, you do whatever you need to do to keep payroll going so that you can support those twenty to one hundred employees whose mortgages depend on you making good decisions. It's very difficult to take a step back and look at risk and security when you don't even know if you're going to be around for another two or three months.

FRAMEWORKS AND SMALL BUSINESSES

The idea is, a framework helps small businesses. Frameworks also help large businesses, of course, but they have an especially positive impact on small businesses. With a framework, a small business doesn't have to waste time wondering how to go about assessing risk.

The concept of a framework will help answer a few key questions and outline, at least from a triage perspective, what you need to pay attention to now so that you and your small business can live to the next day.

To take the triage analogy further, if I have a gunshot wound but also have high cholesterol, what do you think I am going to spend money on first? I am going to stop the bleeding.

For small to midsize businesses, we also advocate a framework that can be created and used without necessarily having an expert. You don't need a superhero.

Still, whether or not you have a superhero, you certainly have a bean counter—even if that's you—and budget realities. It's easy to go through this triage process, and the first thing an organization realizes is, "Oh my God, I need everything."

When budget isn't a problem, you can have everything. But if you want a Ferrari but only have money for a Chevette, how do you decide what features to buy and how to go about it? The decisions that you should make around these budget realities include triaging correctly to decide which features are inside the Chevette that you can actually afford that will take you and your company down the road.

TIERS AND FEATURES OF FRAMEWORKS

Most frameworks are broken up into three different features— activities, standards, and pillars—that you have to take into consideration while using it. These are the framework's core.

This means, here are all of the activities, here are all of the standards, here are all of the pillars. These are the core things that you need to think about as far as cybersecurity goes

After this, there are implementation tiers. In the NIST Cybersecurity Framework, these regard the question, "How well am I doing each of these core things?" In this part of the framework, you must also consider methodology around how the core activities and core standards will be measured in order to determine your effective level of each.

The last part is the framework profile. This is what most executives are interested in. On its own, having a core set of things that you're supposed to be doing and then understanding how well you're doing them does not really help the C-level suite. You need a framework profile, which ties this whole thing back into the actual business case or business functions. Those are the three key things that need to be in each framework.

So when you're looking to choose a framework, if you go with NIST, it will be implementation tiers. If you go with something else, look for a mature core supported by industry standards, and then tie that core directly into what your industry is trying to accomplish.

Make sure you have implementation tiers so that you can assess how well you are doing in each core activity. Also, ensure that there's a way to tie the framework back into a profile that can demonstrate business value.

UNDERSTANDING FRAMEWORK TIERS

There are ways to review the tiers the NIST Cybersecurity Framework uses. When you're going out and looking to try to find a framework to adopt, they should follow our points below:

Tier 1 is manual. You are doing the best you can in implementing a core activity, but you really don't have a plan, and you actually have no idea if you're being effective. At best, you are improvising.

Tier 2 is risk partial. This means you know where the important stuff is when you're taking steps to protect them, but you don't have a broad scope. You still don't have a very clear idea where the organization is. Here, you're basically locking the doors to the important parts of the building, but you don't know what's going on with the rest of it to give a physical point of view.

Tier 3 is repeatable. That means you have formal processes and procedures. You have an organization-wide point of view, with processes, procedures, and best practices updated as the business grows and changes. They are not static but instead dynamic, along with the company. This is the tier where organizations begin to look at what they're doing when interacting with other organizations.

Tier 4, the last and most advanced tier, is adaptive. This is where your cybersecurity practices are mature enough and you're getting enough intelligence from your cybersecurity technology and processes that you are able to follow a pattern of lessons learned. You have proactive indicators for what is going on in the environment. You're like a pilot, flying the cybersecurity environment by instruments and dashboards, so that you can see what's going on. You can be trending and finding analysis that allow you to make better decisions.

Everything you're going to do inside of a framework is going to sit within these four tiers. You might also have different tiers for different core parts of a framework, so that x activity might be at Tier 2 while y activity is at Tier 4.

To build your maturity level model and to build the right profile, it is very important to assess each of these tiers. You must find out where your core framework functionality exists and then look at what is necessary to move from one tier to another.

Large, well-known companies have their own way of going about the framework and the tier systems. They have systems and programs in place and use specific software. IBM uses a product called XGS, a smart firewall. It sits on your network within the mess of the network's interactions with twenty thousand other companies. When it detects a risk, all this data feeds back to the cyber experts in the IBM hive.

When those experts detect a problem or a risk or a new threat, they proactively create a solution and push it out to the others. The theory is that just as there are zero day viruses and threats, the large companies have zero day resolutions—meaning that they can respond quickly to any risk they see.

That to us is protection. Protection is working with the right group of people, understanding how we need to protect what assets are possible, and coming up with an elegant solution that has an automated response to a threat.

The people we know who do it best are IBM with XGS and Palo Alto with their smart firewalls. But these are large companies, with very large amounts of money and resources. Still, they can serve as models for smaller companies of where they want to go.

TIERS AND YOUR INDIVIDUAL COMPANY EXPERIENCE

Looking at all of this, it may seem that you have to be Tier 4 on everything. But sometimes the money it costs to get to Tier 4 on every single cybersecurity practice is not in line with business needs. There might not be a cost benefit.

That's where that profile is very important, aligning security practices with business needs, because you can waste a lot of money and get a very pretty spreadsheet that shows you all of the cybersecurity maturity you have, but if you only need a Chevette, don't buy a Ferrari. It's a lot of fun to drive, but it's also really expensive.

Our framework is designed so that you can go through the process of figuring out what you need to do just by using the framework. This can also be done by someone in HR, finance, or another division if your company is too small to have an actual security staff person. That's the beauty of it.

Now that you have figured out what you own and what is mission critical, it's time to take a look at how to protect it.

ASSESSING WHERE YOU ARE IN THE FRAMEWORK TIER SYSTEM

Now that you know more about tiers, how do you know what tier you are currently in? Do any of these situations sound like you? You might be in that tier!

Tier #1: Manual

"We have a guy who walks around and looks at the hardware that people are using, and we have some spreadsheets that keep track of the stuff they are using. We are really good about putting the asset tags into the spreadsheet when we give it out, and we track who the hardware is assigned to."

"It would take me a lot of time to tell you what software people have on their computers or what is installed on our servers."

"I have some network diagrams of what we are using and where the stuff is on the network, but I would have to go to each switch to understand what patch level they are on."

"I understand the risks that my company faces, and I know what compliance-related data looks like. I can get the auditors what they need, and we do this through a large effort where our IT people go around and gather it up."

Tier #2: Partial

"We have some software that keeps track of all of our physical assets, and we use it as much as possible. We have some policies in place to make sure new devices and software coming into our environment is tracked."

"We have one or more products that help us with asset management, inventory, and detecting what is running on our assets."

"When the auditors come knocking, we run reports off of our software and provide them with that. Anything that is lacking we gather by hand."

Tier #3: Repeatable

"We have policies and procedures that are documented and software that is configured to those documents around asset management, inventory, and monitoring."

"We have automated processes in place for gathering the asset data and creating alerts when violations occur."

"We have a systematic approach to creating auditing data and work with our auditors to empower them."

Tier #4: Adaptive

"We have scheduled strategy sessions to identify trends and future asset initiatives inside the company and use this data to assess if our policies, procedures, and tactics are appropriate for the direction of the company."

"We are plugged into industry regulations and understand future compliance burdens that will be placed on our asset management, inventory, and monitoring tactics."

"We have a systematic way to review projects and issues around understanding our assets."

"We use a combination of lessons learned from our past and the direction of our company and our industry to create our asset management strategies."

"We are empowered to change direction based on new data."

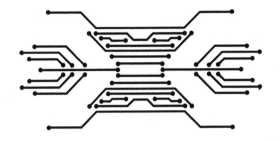

CHAPTER 5

FRAMEWORK PRINCIPLE 2: HOW DO YOU PROTECT ASSETS?

From the NIST Cybersecurity Framework Document:

Protect. *Develop and implement the appropriate safeguards to ensure delivery of critical infrastructure services. The Protect function supports the ability to limit or contain the impact of a potential cybersecurity event. Examples of outcome categories within this function include: access control; awareness and training; data security; information protection processes and procedures; maintenance; and protective technology.*

P rotecting assets is a multifunctional process. We must deal with various topics, including access control, awareness and training, data security, informational process and procedures, maintenance, and protective technology, among other possible issues.

Most companies do the first three things extremely well through the process of identifying, protecting, and detecting. They do these things well because there are vendors and software packages out there that will help them.

Once a company has a solid understanding of the targets they are trying to protect, it can easily find software products that can do it. Among the issues you are looking at is access control, as well as promoting awareness among your staff to be on the alert for things that can go wrong.

As director of security, you, along with the higher-ups within the company, must ask yourself, "How do I go about allowing only those people I determine should have access to important assets?"

ACCESS AND PROTECTION METHODOLOGY

When we talk to people about asset protection, we tell them that there is a methodology they need to follow. First, they need to be aware of the business model of their company, and then they need to protect the business model because the framework has given them a giant blueprint of every single asset.

Not all blueprints are created equal, however. Typically, our IT people create solutions based on what can happen or on what they find interesting at the time they are putting recommendations together. That doesn't always translate back into business knowledge. Asset awareness has something to do with business, of course, but it is in drawing the bigger picture of the business where IT's interaction is most important.

This chapter is about prioritizing and triaging the assets that require the most care and feeding for protection. The question you must be asking yourself is "How do I determine what assets I need to control and protect?"

Our previous chapter discusses risk assessment in great detail. Those points will help you focus where you need to train. Training must be focused, of course, because you cannot train all of your employees on every single security threat that they might encounter.

WHERE IS THE ATTACK MOST LIKELY, AND WHAT FORM IS IT IN?

This year (2015), we've consulted with one large company client on the most likely way that they might get hacked. The literature tells us that currently, the most likely vector is a phishing or spear-phishing email to a senior executive, using something that looks like a normal email, often with a link. Therefore, the focus of our training is on who is most likely to be targeted.

The incidents at Sony show that you have a responsibility to educate your C-suite on how those risks came about for that entertainment company. We use the very vivid example of the break in that so embarrassed Sony, assumed to be by North Korea, in our communication with the executive level. It is something in the news that the C-suite understands and does not want to happen. What we try to do is to put the circumstances into language that senior executives can understand, allowing them to decide what the takeaways are from the Sony hack.

It might seem fatalistic, but the truth is that no company can use only technology to protect itself from a highly focused, highly skilled attack. Bruce Schneier, who's an acknowledged information security expert, talks about risk as a graph with two axes, Focus and Skill. A highly skilled and highly focused attack is virtually impossible to protect against.[4]

That is essentially what happened with Sony. Sony was specifically targeted. This was nothing new for the company, as they've been targeted by other groups for years. Their gaming network, for example, was hacked a few years ago. The North Korean attack was not even Sony Pictures Entertainment's first 2014 hack. There had already been one earlier that year.

Sony was specifically targeted by people who were highly skilled. No company can withstand that. A typical company today, if they do the bare minimum in cybersecurity, is probably protected from a low focus, low skill attack.

If you are a small or medium-sized company and you have some antivirus protection along with firewalls, then you can withstand the drive-bys, the guys walking down the street checking the door handles. They are not really focused, nor are they really skilled.

The highly skilled attacks from people using advanced system threats are another story. If they are using sophisticated tools as persistent threats in a random way, not really focused on your company, that is where you have an opportunity in your company.

No one is really prepared to handle highly skilled attacks, even including the US government, which itself has suffered from hacks. We have tried to craft a message that says to upper management,

---

4 Schneier, Bruce. 2014. "Sony Made It Easy, But Any of Us Could Get Hacked." Wall Street Journal, December 19.

"Listen, we can spend a lot of money, and you might think we can protect ourselves from a Sony-style attack, but we really can't." But we can certainly protect ourselves from the types of things that happened to Home Depot or Target.

SEGMENTING RISK

An important part of this is that Sony was deeply penetrated by the hackers and had a deep exposure. Still, there were key points of intellectual capital that the hackers did not have access to because Sony's IT specialists segmented the company's risk.

Having the emails from chief executives leak out is embarrassing as hell. But it is not as embarrassing as the Playstation 5 confidential product schematics or other trade secrets being leaked. Despite the negative press the company endured, we are still big fans of Sony's CISO because there was a segmentation of risk planned within the larger organization.

The important thing about segmentation of assets is that it allows a deferral of risk. That is the mantra of today's security professional. We cannot keep people out, but we can make sure that once they get in, they cannot get access to the things we do not want them to get access to. There is hope!

Now, on the flip side, one problem with segmentation is that it can get in the way of companies concerned with innovation and creativity. Such companies go out of their way to foster communication across business lines and outside of the company. Anything that slows down collaboration is a threat to innovation. One of the challenges is figuring out how to protect the assets without stifling communication, creativity, or business value. With companies where creativity is paramount, we sometimes use the M&M analogy: a super-hard outer shell, and then a very loose access control inside to allow for maximum collaboration.

Network segmentation is a case where if we are trying to protect certain data that is high risk for interruption, such as R&D information, then we never allow those assets on a network. With segmentation, the bad guys might be able to breach the system, getting into some rooms, so to speak, but the really valuable stuff is in a different area.

There are multiple levels of protecting the assets in the right way. In many ways, it has nothing to do with technology per se. It has to do with understanding processes, procedures, business value, and how to track it back.

That might all sound super boring to a layperson. We also feel like we repeat the same thing over and over. The major risk to organizations isn't that they have the wrong technology in place. The major risk is when processes and procedures are too complex to audit—or they are not complex enough, meaning that somebody who gets in has access to everything.

As an example of a procedure that helps protect assets, at one global company we previously worked with we didn't let our senior executives go to China with the same laptop with which they log into our network. Instead, they received a special travel laptop because we knew those laptop endpoints were going to get attacked as soon as they connected to Chinese infrastructure.

WHEN PROTECTING ISN'T REALLY PROTECTING: THE SPECIAL CASE OF LAPTOPS

Clearly, knowing all there is to know about Chinese hacking methods, it's important to be cautious about laptop usage when traveling there. Still, at times we can get so focused on the looseness and portability of laptops that we focus on the wrong thing.

Take the case of one manufacturing company with about twenty thousand employees in North America. Most are factory workers who do not need laptops, but they have approximately 11,500 laptops out in the inventory. From time to time, employees lose their laptops, or they get stolen while traveling. For a long time, the company had no clue how many laptops were getting lost.

There was no central way to capture that data. Additionally, for most of us in the information security field, it is really not the dollar value of the laptop that we are concerned about. It's the information on the laptop.

The company security team got together to analyze the current process and said, "How can we figure out definitively when a laptop gets stolen?" For the most part, over the years, it was only by chance that they might hear about it. If the laptop was lost at the corporate HQ, they might have heard about it from the IT department, but the company has salespeople who work from home, scattered all over North America.

The company said, "Well, what's the process? How do we issue laptops, and if someone needs a new laptop, how do they get it?"

The answer to that question at the time was that if someone lost his or her laptop or the device got stolen, they had to call the IT support help desk. In that old process, an employee could lose a laptop, call the help desk, and get a new one. No manager would be notified in the process.

The company's security specialists decided, "We don't like that process, and we want visibility on what is lost, so what we're going to do is change the script at the help desk." Now if somebody calls the help desk and requests a new laptop, the script was changed to say, "Well, you need a case number from the corporate security office before we can continue." The security team added a step into the process.

So now when losing a laptop, before the employee can get a new one, he or she has to contact the security department. The process now includes providing the details of the laptop, where it was stolen, and so on, and receiving a case number. Only then can that person go back to the help desk and get his or her laptop.

With this new process, that company has complete visibility, and with this visibility they can make sound decisions about how to address the risk associated with lost laptops potentially full of company secrets.

The highlight here is that it is important to understand how the process works in order to find the right kind of response to it. Typically, if you're just saying, "Hey, I need to protect my laptop," and you go out and you "ready, shoot, aim," you're going to buy something you don't need, or you're going to provide new processes and procedures that are going to make everything more complicated.

Instead, when you really look at the process flow in this example, it's an elegant solution. What this company did was simply change what the help desk was doing. There was no purchase of any expensive new tracking software. This also highlights that cybersecurity is about human interaction and processes and procedures, not technology.

At the same time, this company had another issue with laptops for which it found a resolution. For the last few years, the company had not had a single laptop stolen from its facilities. Every stolen laptop had instead been taken from an employee's car or had been lost by an employee while traveling.

Looking at where laptops were stolen, the company said, "Listen, you don't have to spend $40 on a laptop locking cable to lock your laptop to your office desk anymore." That workplace requirement, which was cumbersome, expensive, and unnecessary, was removed. However, for employees traveling or using the laptop at a café, for example, the company's best practice continued to be using a locking cable, as that is where the risk of being stolen lies.

The company also analyzed other laptop procedures which they decided were cumbersome and got in the way of work. For example, the company used to require a permission slip to remove a laptop from the office. The building security also did random bag checks. When an employee left the office, the physical security staff in the lobby would make sure that he or she wasn't taking somebody else's laptop out of the office.

So the employee had a little permission slip, signed by the manager, that had the asset tag number of his or her laptop. The security guy was supposed to look at the little permission slip and compare the number on there to the number on the actual laptop you were carrying out of the building.

These permission slips had to get updated every year. It was costing the company 1.75 full-time equivalents per year between two sites to accomplish that process. The company decided simply to eliminate that process, as there was no problem with people stealing laptops from work. The process was unnecessary and costly and actually got in the way of productivity.

This laptop process was, to use a common phrase about airports, good security theater, but it added nothing in actuality to real security.

And, indeed, other than the information that might be on a laptop, the actual device is cheap to replace if lost or stolen.

TAILORED SECURITY

All of this process around laptops also shows that we are not advocating more security, more security, more security all the time. We're saying, "Tailor the security." Tailor what you are doing as a security manager to what the true risks are for your company.

Additionally, tailor the appropriate response. In this way, the processes and procedures are around the response. That might not be a technology solution but rather a human one, or one of process, as with the laptops.

However, an additional issue arises when data is stolen via a laptop or other portable device—not just that the data is stolen and now someone has to deal with it. If data is stolen and you no longer have access to it, what is the opportunity loss for not having your laptops backed up in a way that you can get to the data?

So, in this dialogue around laptops, focus number one is on the physical device and keeping it with you. Number two is how do we protect the data if it gets out of our hands? We might choose hard drive encryption, passwords, and other technology solutions so that whoever gets the laptop cannot read what is inside.

And three, how do we maintain possession of intellectual capital if it's only on that particular laptop? So how are we doing backups? How are we tracking those backups? Looking at this really does come down to understanding what you are trying to accomplish, what your key business objectives are, and how you actually do business.

All of this is why laptops are indeed a special case. But there is a need for them to be looked at logically and in a way that allows them to do what they are supposed to do, which is to make it easier to work anywhere at any time for your employees.

UNDER CONSTANT BARRAGE, THE BORING STUFF MUST STILL BE ACCOMPLISHED

Heartbleed is just one example of a form of hacking or attack, and one with a very catchy name. But there's a constant barrage of things that pop up that we have to react to. Another attack was called "Bad USB." Some bad guys figured out how to rewrite firmware on a USB stick. It could do bad things that your antivirus wouldn't pick up on.

Then there was "Dark Hotel," which was a covert, Russian-led effort to collect information on high-level people logging into hotel Wi-Fi networks. Heartbleed, Dark Hotel, Bad USB—all catchy names for quite sinister things that can happen to your systems. If they were called something like SSL Vulnerability Exploit, no one would pay any attention, except for us systems nerds.

These attacks have largely targeted Windows-based systems, but recently a new attack called Thunderstrike has been targeting MacBooks, Mac OS, and systems with a Thunderbolt interface. If you look at informational processes and procedures up to this point, most of us thought that Windows was the risky environment.

We make decisions on cybersecurity and physical security based on such assumptions. But the fact is that we are always lagging behind the hackers. They are on constant lookout for opportunities. So everyone thought, "Hey, I've got an iOS device. I'm safe," because everyone's hacking open source Android instead.

The main objective with informational processes and procedures is to have a better understanding of how they are used in your company. It all comes back to what the company is doing now that's innovative and interesting. We talked earlier about how business innovation outpaces security.

In security, we typically work on the back 80 percent of business value, and we do not get to participate in the front 20 percent.

Going by the 80/20 rule, where 20 percent of innovation provides 80 percent of the value, what we are doing is locking in 20 percent of the value by protecting 80 percent of the legacy assets. That is a mistake, and it is very dangerous if we do not approach it in the right way.

The interesting part about the protection aspect of the framework is that it really does help you make decisions. Where should I spend my money in a way that protects 80 percent of the value, rather than the traditional 20 percent?

This is important. This is the stuff that lets companies do bold things, grab new markets, and retain the value they created.

Anyone can create value. Retaining that value is the role of cybersecurity.

MAINTENANCE:
BORING BUT IMPORTANT

Maintenance is the next aspect of protection. This is the most boring part of information technology. It is also the most undervalued, unless somebody doesn't do it.

But here's the catch—and it's important to understand because of these surprises that come up. IT is all about "what have you done for me lately." When I say nothing's gone wrong in five years, the company's executives might come back and say, "Well, that's very boring, and I can't get funding for it."

The reason why the Heartbleed malware was successful was because it exploited people who hadn't updated their servers to the latest encryption technology. They had not done anything lately, and that is what left them vulnerable. You must have upkeep, even if it is boring. You have to spend resources to keep your systems patched and your firewall rules up to date.

The challenge is growing more difficult as businesses become more fast paced and technology changes more quickly. Your hardware environment and your application environment will change, maybe without you even knowing about it.

It goes back to the inventory issue. People in different parts of your business are just doing things, attaching things to the network. But how do you find out about it?

For example, one company we work with found out its factory in Canada had attached a vending machine to its network. Apparently soda and candy machines are network devices now. It was shocking to us to find out that these guys had incorporated this onto the network so that the vending machine could phone home and tell the vending company when it ran out of Snickers bars. Certainly, this makes getting snacking supplies easier, but it also opens a huge number of vulnerabilities for the company.

This kind of risk into the system happens now all over the environment, as more and more systems become integrated. The point is, maintenance is a challenge. It is a boring, expensive thing that you have to do because if you don't, typically that is how you're going to get taken out. That was what Heartbleed was all about.

REACHING THE END ZONE

Now let me give you an analogy on maintenance from the world of college football. There was a football player from the University of Florida named Emmett Smith, who became a low-profile running back for the Dallas Cowboys. Now, why did he have a successful career? Was he a gifted running back? Absolutely. Was he an amazing athlete? Without a question. But the true reason he was a good running back who could get five-plus yards on every run was because his defensive line moved and made holes for him.

For business systems, this basic blocking and tackling is what maintenance is. Maintenance is a boring blocking and tackling function that allows new and exciting innovation to gain yardage.

The thing that folks don't realize is that if you don't invest in maintenance, if you don't invest in your boring protection of assets, if you can't find a way to allocate the resources necessary to have the best offensive line that the whole league has ever seen, then it does not matter how gifted your innovation is or how talented your running back is. You are not going to reach the end zone.

That is why framework is key for a small or midsize company. The framework provides a profile in a soft process around how you pick your starting lineup. Do you understand what your blocking and tackling needs look like? How do you take your business concerns and put them in such a way that you can pick the right team?

In general, frameworks allow you to understand where you are trying to go with a business and what the assets are that are going to take you there, and knowing all of this allows you to protect those assets.

If we go back to the football analogy of "Hey, what is the goal?"— that's easy, it's the end zone. The asset that is going to take you there is the running back. The protection in that process is asking ourselves, how do we make sure the running back gets to run? That's the blocking and tackling.

Additionally, it's about triage, making sure to ask yourself, "Where do I need to invest the most?" Every large company can have a thousand plays in the playbook. A small company can probably have two—so when you're investing in blocking and tackling, you're investing in systems that protect those two particular plays.

A framework is essential for helping you figure that all out.

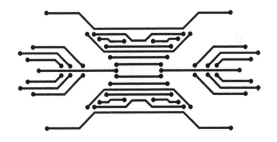

CHAPTER 6

FRAMEWORK PRINCIPLE 3:
HOW DO YOU DETECT THREATS?

From the NIST Cybersecurity Framework Document:

Detect. *Develop and implement the appropriate activities to identify the occurrence of a cybersecurity event. The Detect function enables timely discovery of cybersecurity events. Examples of outcome categories within this function include: anomalies and events; security continuous monitoring; and detection processes.*

We know that asset management is very important, and understanding what you have and knowing thyself is the first step. When you get to the Detect principle, which is the technology part of the Framework, you now have some knowledge of what you might be looking for.

This is typically when you will be working with the antivirus folks on your team. You look at monitoring to determine what is actually happening on devices. You also take a step up in the complexity of the technology you're using.

The way to build a monitoring or a tech strategy is to look at what your key business functions are. Take the retail example. If we're concerned about our supply chain, our point of sales, and our financial transactions, then we need to make sure that all those systems are secure.

So now we have quantified the assets, we know where all these things are, and we know how they work. Now we have to apply the right detection strategies, according to priority.

DEATH BY MONITORING

There is also the difference between point checking and continuous monitoring to consider. One caution, of course, is what we call "death by monitoring." When you first go into monitoring, you say, "I'd like to know everything about everything. I want to put an agent on every single endpoint, and I want to collect as much data as possible, and I want to know it all. I want to know if anything happens, any hiccups." That idea is indeed a fantastic, noble one.

Unfortunately, what happens is that now you have a flood of data. You get death by monitoring. You can cripple your endpoints with software that's grabbing so much information. In addition, you need to have human beings who actually can process this flood of information.

You have to align the technology that you want to use with your ability to consume the data. This must be done while being mindful of the impact you will have on the performance of the systems you are trying to monitor.

Typically what happens is that instead of having 100 percent monitoring all of the time on every single function and feature, there's a prioritization process that goes on. Then you may begin to ratchet back in some areas as you examine the process.

It turns out you may only need to check some logs once a week because certain areas are very low risk. On the other hand, there might be other data points that are so critical that you need to check them every fifteen minutes or whatever the best case might be.

The Target data breach is a horror story in the human side of monitoring. They were using a tool to detect advanced threats from a company called FireEye, and it actually detected that they were being hacked. However, the Target guys monitoring this either did not look at their logs or perhaps figured it was not important enough to investigate further.

What begins to happen is that when you turn logging on for everything, the logs are never looked at. Then, the only thing that some IT professionals are worried about is when the logs fill up disk space. That results in a problem ticket going off in the middle of the night, where you've got to get into the system to delete some logs.

Logging, in our opinion, is the best friend of the hard disk industry, because we keep all this information and do not know what to do with it. It is detection without intelligence—without knowing why we are even doing it.

NEW PRODUCTS AND LEARNING CURVES

All of this can be difficult to get a hold on, though, especially if you are just getting a new product. With something new, you often have no idea where to start, and there will be a learning curve. You are either going to pay handsomely to some consultant to come in and help you build your strategy, or you will have to be okay with some lessons learned and a few bloody noses. There's no silver bullet. It can be a painful process getting your monitoring and detection down right.

This is why executive sponsorship and getting people on board with what you are trying to accomplish is very important. Tying this back into a priority which is aligned with business will allow that to happen.

There are a few ways to get support on what we need done. At one large client we consult with, a key business driver is the intellectual property they use to create and differentiate their products. On a recent call, we discussed the specific IT systems that control the confidential recipes for the various types of production materials that they use. Just before that, we had a call reviewing the network diagrams for these systems because we were detecting someone scanning the network for vulnerabilities.

It was a malicious attempt to find weaknesses on the network, so we said, "Hey, we need to take a fresh look at the network topology and the firewall rules, to ensure that everything's up-to-date." However, that might not be something we can do for everything on the network. We only focus on critical assets, as otherwise it would cost too much money. We would have to hire too many people to do everything.

We see with many things happening recently—at Target and at Sony, for example—that even multibillion-dollar companies are not able to monitor everything in a way that they would like. We always want more data. We should always want better data.

Hearing about the problems of the big guys with seemingly unlimited resources, we can see how small businesses must believe that they have no chance whatsoever. They must believe that, "Hey, if these big guys can't do it, well, I'm screwed." The good news, though, is that it is much easier to secure a small business than a large business.

And we will tell you the reason.

It is simply because of the sheer and inherent complexity of large businesses—the amount of moving parts and interdependencies. These can cause blind spots. The advantage of a small business's processes and procedures, and how they do what they do, is that everything is so much easier to identify. Once you have that, you can apply cybersecurity in the right way.

There are lessons from how large companies run their detection and monitoring initiatives that can be applied to a small business, far more efficiently and for far less money. The problem that a detection strategy has is that when it's working, nobody's impressed. But when it fails, that's when people give it—and you—attention.

DEFINING WHAT YOU'RE MONITORING

Defining upfront what the success and failure of a detection system and methodology should be is important because very frequently folks do not understand what they are buying or what their strategy is supposed to accomplish. When you tell somebody, "Oh yes, we're monitoring that device," they assume that you are monitoring everything about the device.

In reality, we may only be monitoring the top five most important things. We might be monitoring disk space. We might be monitoring who has logged into the system, or whatever at your company you deem is the priority. Yet in trying not to have a massive flood of data no one can do anything with, coupled with our prioritization process, we do leave ourselves exposed in such a way that there are things to which we are just not paying attention.

Back in my early twenties, long before I started Palmetto, when I was first setting up systems and still learning, I can remember waking up in the middle of the night because my pager (remember those?) was always going off. The company I was working for at the time was running out of disk space on the AIX UNIX boxes.

At the time, all I knew how to do was to just delete stuff. I did not know how to really look at the logs. By not having a proactive detection strategy, everything recorded is going to consume the diskspace. This is all part of the learning process. It was not until I turned twenty-four that I started writing my own code to go through and monitor these logs, because the data in the logs is the whole secret sauce of what's going on—performance issues, threats, everything.

This of course signifies why it is so important to understand what is in the logs and to prioritize that information. Detection is not just the software and the processes and procedures that live in these devices. It is also the ability to report on them. For example, if you have automated detection, but it has no way to actually reach out and tell an IT professional when something's going on, it's pretty useless.

Tight integration with problem resolution is also about changing the management of software. For example, Remedy is the name of one such choice. Another is SIEM, which is a tool that brings all of these different detection tools into one dashboard.

DISCUSSING PRIORITIZATION WITH MANAGEMENT

When you are prioritizing, you will talk to the line of business, the people in marketing, and other divisions at your company. You will ask them their priorities, saying, "What do I need to monitor?" and they're going to respond back, "Everything."

Then the best thing you can do—the way that we have had the most success with prioritization—is getting everybody in a room, sitting face-to-face. Then, the question IT people should be asking isn't "Tell me about your environment." Instead, you should ask, "Explain to me the process flow of how people are going to use this technology."

Once you understand human behavior and how that human behavior is going to be applied to the line of business, you start making detection decisions based on what the humans are doing. You can then point out which human behavior is actually being tracked.

If this or that is being put into a particular log book, we need to know if it is going to be generating data. If it's generating data, it means we need to look at the disk space.

This information reconnaissance with staff goes to the question, "How do you prioritize what you're going to look at?" You need to know what your critical systems are that your business can't live without. Since you can't look at everything, you must know what the high priority systems are.

After this, the second thing you need to understand is the threats you are most likely going to face. You must understand where the threats are coming from. For example, antivirus logs are not very important anymore. There is much more sophisticated malware now that is more likely to hack through, as opposed to your run-of-the-mill virus. Therefore, two ways that you can help prioritize are (1) knowing what the true threats are today and (2) knowing what your critical systems are at your company.

Perhaps we can relate best to an example in the analog world. When you go to bed at night, you make sure the front door is locked and the back door is locked, but you don't check the upstairs windows every night. That's not likely to be where the threat is coming from.

And whether it's locking doors or protecting systems at your company, you'll sleep better at night either way.

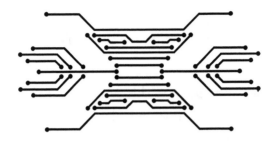

CHAPTER 7

FRAMEWORK PRINCIPLE 4: HOW DO YOU RESPOND? / WHAT IS THE RESPONSE PLAN?

From the NIST Cybersecurity Framework Document:

Respond. *Develop and implement the appropriate activities to take action regarding a detected cybersecurity event. The Respond function supports the ability to contain the impact of a potential cybersecurity event. Examples of outcome categories within this function include: response planning; communications; analysis; mitigation; and improvements.*

Let's take a look back at the last few steps from previous chapters. You've determined how people are using the systems, and you've figured out what you'll be monitoring based on your budget. You're now monitoring, and you've detected something going on.

Now we want to respond to this. What could happen? What are some of the different scenarios, and what are some of the communication processes that would occur?

For the response to be effective, there has to be a system that allows you to categorize your risks and threats in such a way that you can respond in an efficient and timely manner. We use levels one through four to evaluate how severe what we have detected is and if it warrants a response. Let's say that we have a level four—we've detected something that's going wrong, but we know enough about our environment and our threats to say it's not really important. We don't have to get to it immediately.

Or, a noncritical system in a lab environment might have some odd login activity, perhaps someone forgetting password indications a few times over. We probably won't be concerned about that, either, because we know developers use that system. On the other hand, say we see something that looks like a denial of service attack on the outside, and at the same time we have one thousand filled logins on two of the UNIX boxes that are Internet-facing. If we start seeing these patterns or we have a system down that is a critical piece of our infrastructure, the situation may be level one, and it's time to get people out of bed.

There are other examples fitting with our framework. In my own company, Palmetto, everyone is a computer expert, so they often fix their own issues. The only things I might care about are signs that someone has gotten inside: weird emails going around (showing that someone clicked on a phishing attack) or tampering on our webpage.

KEEPING CLIENTS INFORMED

Our key concerns are in how we deal with our customers. So, for us, the response in our detection and all of our security is focused around touchpoints with our clients and what we are doing with their data.

Take laptops, for example. If we lost a laptop, how would we respond? If a customer gave us data and we put it on a secure laptop and then we got on a plane and left the laptop in the overhead bin, well, how would we respond? It's not the value of the laptop that matters—whether it's a cheap $200 model or a fancy $2,000 unit loaded with expensive features. It's the value of the information in the laptop. This is key for people in your company to understand. It is something that could impact the company's bottom line.

Beyond that, it is not just a matter of repairing or going after the laptop and trying to recover it. You must also notify your clients. You have to let them know about a potential compromise. The important part of the response step is determining who needs to know so that they can make intelligent decisions around what just happened. And I think that is the core to how we approach this.

Now, if you are going to respond, it's important also to have a process around that. Since it can potentially involve contacting your clients about an issue, the response has to be well thought out, sensitive, and properly communicated by people responsible for that communication.

So, for example, when there is an issue or an incident, who is responsible? Who is the point person who leads and communicates through this for the company?

You may not have a written plan, but if you are a small business you at least have someone who knows that one of his or her duties is to respond to cybersecurity incidents.

There also must be someone who communicates to client companies whose information is on that laptop. You have to take responsibility for the mistake and let the client know that their company or employees might be at risk because of the lost laptop.

Quite clearly, this is what makes companies shiver. A security compromise may put your company's reputation at risk. That is certainly something to worry about, but you must address the issue head on so that clients know you are addressing it. Not doing so would be far worse.

If you were in a larger company, there would be more human beings involved and more processes and procedures. But no matter the size of the company, someone must be held accountable and responsible for ensuring follow through.

LOOKING AT THE DATA DURING A COMPROMISE

There are three things we talk about when considering data and how sensitive it is. The first is confidentiality, the next is availability, and the third is integrity. Integrity refers specifically to integrity of the data—you want to make sure that no one has changed your data, such as numbers on spreadsheets.

How you respond is also based on asking, "What's your objective?" If you are concerned about the availability of a certain system, then you need to have good backups, and you must decide how often that should occur. Maybe you need daily backups for certain systems, and maybe you need backups minute by minute for very critical data points. You might also need to have mirrored systems, in case your system is so critical that you would have to keep this machine alive to continue in business. In such a case, if the machine gets corrupted, you might need to have another machine that can instantly take over that process.

One of the important parts of the respond step is disclosure to the stakeholders and business partners. You want to do this in such a way that you and all those invested in the issue understand what happened, and then you can go over the lessons learned together. Other components of this are forming answers to the questions, "How do we respond better as a company?" and "How do we take this up to the executive level in order to resolve particular process issues?" There are people throughout your organization who are going to have an opinion, and those opinions won't always align. So the next steps often require an executive to make a decision.

In such cases, not being silent is very important. If you have a breach or a problem and only your organization learns from it, then the overall cybersecurity ecosystem suffers.

Here is where we will go back to peer groups. We are not saying post the problem on your company's blog, which is almost like taking an airplane to skywrite, "We've been hacked. Great. This is what they did to us." Instead, it's about getting together with a confidential group of other cybersecurity or physical security professionals, or security professionals in general, to say, "This is what happened. This is how we responded to it."

When you don't learn from an event, then it will happen again. Perhaps not everything deserves a deep postmortem, but you should look at every event that comes across your table to at least make that decision.

LEARNING FROM TYLENOL

We'll give you an example, although it's from the analog world. It's about the Tylenol tampering that occurred in 1982, where someone placed cyanide into the product and several people died.

This had nothing to do with Tylenol's procedures or manufacturing processes leading to contamination. It was someone tampering with the product on store shelves. This was disastrous for Tylenol. However, rather than assign blame or hide from the public, the company faced the crisis head on, recalling all products and dealing in an open manner with the media and the public. This was done in line with Johnson & Johnson's mission statement. When Tylenol was reintroduced, it used triple safety seals to make tampering more difficult and visible if and when it does happen. This system is now used across the board for almost all medicines and some food items. In other words, Tylenol responded quickly and in an open manner, and as a result, we are all safer now. The company also, of course, saved its bottom line, as Tylenol remains one of America's top pain relievers.

This response made the entire industry stronger after the threat, and that is why sharing knowledge and being open is so important.

It also shows how important your public relations team can be in mitigating a disaster.

THE LEFT FIELD ATTACK

Always the most difficult is thinking about what can happen and how we are going to plan for it. It is often frustrating because we simply cannot plan for everything. It can be demoralizing to spend time coming up with a giant plan and then get hit by something out of left field.

We love to encourage people to sit down and at least plan for what they already know about. If we take it to another sports analogy, you will study the other team's plays and look at videos, and you'll see how they're coming at you, and then plan for those particular things. Yes, hackers could bring on something that you've never seen before, but at least you'll have a baseline security response for when something truly horrible happens.

September 11 is such a case. We had a lot of our servers and infrastructure impacted, as did many people throughout the United States. We had to do seventy-two hours nonstop work in order to bring the environments back up. There was no way we could have directly planned for an event of that magnitude and surprise.

However, we had long planned for what would happen if we were to lose our servers and needed to respond quickly in an emergency. We had to modify this existing plan because there was so much more to do than what we were anticipating. Still, because we had something to start with, it allowed us to take action sooner. That's what this is all about.

The time it takes for you to take action and respond to an incident—those moments are precious. This is especially true if somebody has gone into your environment pulling intellectual capital and critical business information out. Having a plan in place could allow you to stop them before they get too far.

Then the analysis of what happened comes after the fact, after you've executed your response. This is the postmortem mentioned earlier—going back and asking why this happened.

Frequently, what larger companies do is have a weekly or daily problem resolution meeting, where everyone involved gets around a table and says, "Hey, what happened last night? Why did it happen? What are you going to do differently next time?"

Such meetings don't often happen in smaller companies. Usually there's an army of one, and he or she says to himself or herself, "Oh wow, I would love to not see that happen again," and then takes action to put out that particular fire

This is another case where peer groups are important. It's very important to have a peer group for large company security people, but it's probably at least as important to have one for the smaller company and the army-of-one security person.

UPPER MANAGEMENT RESPONSIBILITY

It is also important to have a senior person within your company or business—someone with executive authority—involved in the response because that will be how you will get the resources you need. It's that person, not the security person, who essentially owns the problem. If you're going to react rapidly, you need senior executive support because that's where the resources to respond are going to come from.

The executive will also help with the decisions. They may say, "You know what? We don't need to move to a different data center. We can wait two days." That person can own the problem and marshal resources, as well as coordinate timing.

When you get into mitigation, one thing you definitely need executive sponsorship for is the approval of safer architectures. There are ways you can set up your environment that inherently protect you better for an unknown risk. One example is segmenting your network into secure zones to have multiple access points.

Think of it as a car having a crumple zone. If you have different compartments and different barriers inside your network, somebody can get into one spot, but they can't get into another. They have to continuously try to get in, like one door leading to another door. In this way, you have more opportunities to detect threats, intrusions, and other problems.

Let's take the example of a virus getting into the system. If it is on a segmented network, it can't reach the rest of the environment. In such a case, you've contained and mitigated that particular threat. Yes, it is in but only in a limited part of the system.

It is interesting that sometimes the best mitigation comes with an awareness of what threats might be coming your way and configuring yourself to be naturally resistant to them.

THUMBS UP OR THUMBS DOWN

There are many ways to think of mitigation. I'll give you an example from a large company involving a money decision. And thumb drives. People love thumb drives.

I was at a large international trade show, and various vendors were handing out their press kits on free thumb drives. People love these things. At one of the companies I support, employees were using them all over the company. Companies would buy batches of them just for one conference to hand out with all their promotional materials.

This company was swimming in thumb drives, and that comes with a lot of risk, including the risk of losing important data if you leave them lying around. Additionally, these things can get infected when you plug them into different machines.

What the company did was say, "All right. No more thumb drives, except for this one thumb drive that has automatic encryption built into it, which you can't turn off. Oh, by the way, they're about $50." Not cheap by the standards of your ordinary thumb drive, but the company's security chief proposed this to the C-suite as a necessary thing to do. If people really needed the thumb drive, then they would pay the $50 to get it.

What the company discovered was that in general, people were really just using thumb drives out of habit. In many cases, they didn't have a hard requirement for one. That's one example of how a company can mitigate issues. It's creative. It's not a roadblock. It also helps the staff understand the importance of security in their behavior.

This is an example of policy being modified and paired with appropriate technology, while being mindful of human behavior. It's a fantastic example of how you can do cybersecurity and security in general in a way that doesn't interfere with the business. The employees at this company could still get the job done. If it was important enough to them, they'd spend that $50, and nothing would be in the way of their performance.

Importantly, that decision was not made by the IT department. It required board sponsorship, reflecting the fact that it is the board's responsibility to approach cybersecurity and security, not IT's responsibility. IT's responsibility within mitigation is to implement policies and procedures and recommend technologies to achieve those goals. The important thing is that the recommendations about cybersecurity by technologists must still tie into business value. Otherwise, you will likely be told no.

Whether thumb drives, laptops, or company smartphones—the best thing a small business can do is to store nothing of value on these devices. Now, you will always have exceptions. If we're doing CAD drawing on a laptop as a proposal for new business, the files will have to be there, of course. But even in those cases, for basic security, we are finding that going to a large cloud provider like Google or Microsoft is a very safe bet.

The game changes when you're dealing with local data centers and local people offering email as a service. That's not to say that many individual ones might not be fantastic. However, among the reasons people deal with Google and Microsoft is that since these major companies know they are constantly under attack, they are exceedingly vigilant about threats. We cannot say that many smaller companies are the same.

RATING COMPANIES ON CYBERSECURITY

Here's a question to ask yourself: How do you assess a vendor to see if they are a secure partner? This is a growing issue as we continuously rely on business partners to host our data for different purposes. We may be very secure, but how do we know the partner we're sharing our resources with is secure? We're in the process now of developing a tool that will give us visibility into how secure our partners are.

There are many tools available to large enterprises. Large enterprises can afford to do risk assessments and due diligence checks and background checks. They can also go to the prospective company's business site to review whether they are as secure as they say they are.

A small company doesn't have that kind of leverage. A small company is not going to get Google or Microsoft to give them their security data to prove how secure they are, because Google and Microsoft don't care about them from a sales point of view.

This issue of vendor security goes far and wide. For example, at one company's research and development campus, they have approximately two hundred business partners. In various capacities, the partners have access to sensitive R&D data. The company has a great program in place to protect their data, but they have no visibility right now into how their business partners approach security. This is a huge blind spot.

That example shows the complexity and challenges of security for a large company, but the principles apply throughout the business world. The thing to remember in this chapter is to ask yourself, "Can we really identify what success looks like for good response?"

The first thing is that you don't want your plans to interrupt the business. You do not want to interrupt cash flow, for example. And from a compliance perspective, you do not want to break any laws or regulations.

You are successful at recovery, which is discussed in detail in our next chapter, when you reduce the impact to cash flow and business value from external or internal events. An external event, again, is something that goes wrong with the vendor or something that happens in the outside world over which you have no control. An internal event is something that maybe you should have been able to see coming inside your environment. Often it is the behavior of people in your company. In either case, brand damage can be an issue, and that is also part of mitigation.

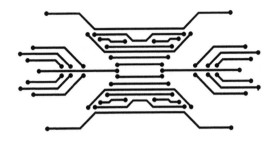

CHAPTER 8

FRAMEWORK PRINCIPLE 5: RECOVERY PLANNING

From the NIST Cybersecurity Framework Document:

Recover. *Develop and implement the appropriate activities to maintain plans for resilience and to restore any capabilities or services that were impaired due to a cybersecurity event. The Recover function supports timely recovery to normal operations to reduce the impact from a cybersecurity event. Examples of outcome categories within this function include: recovery planning; improvements; and communications.*

In this chapter we look at recovery—what to do after a breach or other security incident. This is the final step within the five-point framework.

Say that something has happened and you've got to fix it. A laptop was stolen. The information on that laptop was breached. Now someone has your sensitive data, and that has hurt your company's brand.

Later, the dust has settled, and things are back together again, but your brand is still damaged. The data is out there, and you lost intellectual capital. The recovery planning step, Principle 5 in our framework, is about what to do after the bad things happen and you've responded to them.

For one, do you have a PR firm on standby as spin doctor to communicate to your public?

One real-life example of a recovery plan for one company we worked with recently was not about a computer virus but a human one—the Ebola virus. It's one thing to think of Ebola in the abstract if it is in Africa, but once it was in Dallas, here in North America, we said, "Hey, do we have a pandemic crisis response plan that addresses what we would do?"

It turned out the company had a plan, but it didn't really cover Ebola and the unique things Ebola brings to the table. So, working with the company, we updated the plan, and one of the things we had to address was having the plan state what to do if Ebola reached a crisis level.

We had that company look, for instance, at its computer network bandwidth. If the company needed to tell people not to come to work as part of the Ebola mitigation plan, it needed to have the ability for them to work remotely. That meant looking at whether the company had enough network capacity for six thousand knowledge workers to connect remotely and whether all six thousand needed to be able to connect—maybe it could be limited to decision makers or those divisions directly impacting cash flow.

This is right out of the NIST Framework playbook: "Develop and implement appropriate activities to maintain plans for resilience and to restore any capabilities or services that were impaired due to the event."

So whether it's rebuilding capacity for a major event or another challenge, a recovery plan exercise has to look at exactly what recovery is all about. You have to ask yourself, "How do I get back to a safe state of doing business when I've had a loss of functionality or some other loss due to whatever I'm responding to?" Sometimes a good response has nothing to do with actually repairing and mitigating.

On the other hand, as an example of a bad response, after South Carolina Treasury Department's stolen Social Security numbers incident, their recovery plan was a year of credit protection. That is not a well-thought-out recovery plan.

DISTILLING THE ISSUE

I'll give you an example from a small business point of view, and it's worth drinking a toast to. At Palmetto, we have a wonderful office on downtown Greenville's Main Street. It's right over a moonshine distillery. I walk up the stairs every morning as the mash is cooking with that wonderful smell. It's just a really pleasant experience for me. The downside is, that smell masked the odor of mold in the building, and several employees began to develop respiratory issues.

When we finally saw black mold coming through the ceiling, we knew we had a problem. We had to get out of the building and rip the walls down to the frames. Everyone had to work remotely.

Luckily, everybody had Gmail and laptops, so we did not need to physically be in one space. We dispersed, working from coffee shops and our homes.

The issue was that this went on for three months. It impacted our productivity, and we had less collaboration on projects where it would have made things better. We suffered. There should have been a better plan, but as far as dollars and cents goes, this was the right level of response and recovery from the mold issue.

So whether it's mold or the Ebola virus keeping it germy here, there's a reason to have these plans in place regardless of the size of your company.

CYBER RECOVERY

Now, we're talking a lot about physical issues, but what happens when there is a cybersecurity breach? How does Target or Sony—bless their hearts with those leaked emails about their spoiled actors—actually recover from one of these horrendous breaches?

There are a lot of different things to start looking at, from brand image to personal data of customers, to loss of revenue and loss of intellectual capital.

We do know that once the cat's out of the bag, this is difficult to answer. It's best to be prepared, if possible. Some large companies have a crisis management team on staff at all times. In many cases, this can mean a company is spending resources to develop written plans that become obsolete as soon as they are approved and may not even get pulled out during a crisis anyway.

Smaller companies may not have the luxury of having well-formed crisis response plans. It may be up to you to lead crisis response in an ad hoc manner.

Whatever the size of your company, it is important to pull together the right senior people and manage it, spending resources as necessary. This may involve getting senior business people together in a room to discuss, brainstorm, problem solve, and make decisions.

Who should be on that crisis response team? You want staff from legal and others from marketing and public relations—and definitely IT. Get all of the C-level executives and their effective reports together because recovery isn't an IT function—it's a business function.

As someone heading your IT department, you need to know who in the company needs to get in the room. Get in touch with them and execute a lengthy meeting. We are not talking about one eight-hour day. You're going to be spending weeks in there, talking through the crisis.

That prep work is essential, along with the ability to assess what level of criticality the event is. Not everything is a Sony level breach, so sometimes you don't need that entire suite of executives. Sometimes you just need a due diligence team inside a line of business that works with IT.

As a small crisis example, one of the companies we worked with discovered an employee had obtained the manager's login and password information for the company's online expense reimbursement tool. It's an Oracle system where you claim expenses, attach receipts, and submit. Your manager gets it and reviews it and approves it, and then on the next paycheck, you get the money back. The employee was creating fake expenses, then approving them using his manager's credentials.

Instead of reacting by adding more responsibilities to managers or changing the reimbursement process, the company just added two-factor authentication to the existing process. This is an example of trying to tailor the recovery for minimal business impact. We want to avoid complaints such as "We have a cumbersome business process due to some of the security constraints."

At other times, as with the thumb drive case, you find what the issue is and come up with a solution. Then you find the technology that allows the employees to do the business function. To tell them they just can't do something doesn't help them perform their business function. By mitigating or creating a special process, you can allow them to perform securely.

For small companies in particular, this is a real issue because you have people who wear many hats. You have to think a little more creatively than a big company with a lot of money.

The interesting point is that people assume big companies have a lot of money, but getting budgets for these things can be gruelingly difficult in a large company. Sometimes a small business is more agile and can make better decisions. For instance, since at Palmetto I have twenty employees, if there's a broken process that doesn't seem to be working right, the resolution is that staff walk into my office and tell me.

My response? "Whoa, you're costing me money. I can't get that sailboat I want if we keep doing this, so let's change it." Now, if Tom wants to change a process at his large company, it can take longer and be more difficult.

REDUCING EMPLOYEE FRICTION
WITH SECURITY ISSUES

At companies of any size, it still can be easier to sell risk mitigation when the proposal reduces friction.

As an example of friction, we created a new policy whereby if you had classified data on your laptop, which we labeled "confidential data," you had to encrypt it using special software. Almost no one did because when the software was deployed by the IT department, no instructions were given, and the software was quite complicated.

To reduce friction and increase the security of laptop data, we decided to take the decisions about encrypting out of the employees' hands. We now automatically encrypt the whole hard drive, behind the scenes. The employee doesn't have to do anything, but now everything's encrypted.

We used a tool that was transparent to the laptop user. It's all invisible, with no friction, whether a laptop or a thumb drive. That's the beauty of it. The security is there, almost invisibly.

WHEN CAN WE DECIDE THAT A CRISIS
HAS PASSED AND THAT WE CAN NOW
CONTINUE DOING BUSINESS?

If we look at Sony, how do they know that they've recovered to a point where they're safe? Of course, safety is an illusion in the security world. It is hard to think we will ever truly be safe, but we have to be able to step back at certain points.

If an event happens and you are responding to it, and you're in the middle of a recovery and doing damage control, at some point you have to ratchet people back. They can't be out there doing seventy-two-hour stretches at crisis level over and over again.

How do you identify that you've reached that point? When can you go back to working on strategic things rather than putting out this fire in front of you?

LESSONS LEARNED AND IMPROVEMENT FOR THE NEXT CRISIS

With every crisis, you must also examine the lessons learned. After all, the reality doesn't always go according to plan. Unforeseen things come up. You want to learn from those unforeseen things and build them into your plan when you update it for the next time.

One thing many security professionals agree on is that your recovery planning is your best guess, something you do with the data on hand. You don't want to spend too much time on this, because a lot of what actually happens will be a curveball. But if your plan can help you shave a couple hours off of your recovery and if your plan can help you be more agile in the face of the unknown, then it's worth the time and investment.

After you go through a disaster or other event and there are lessons learned, it's important to take those lessons and put them into the plan or to assess your plan to see if there's anything that needs to change.

That's when improvement comes in. When you have lessons learned, it doesn't do anything to just sit around the table and talk about them. You have to put them into action in some form.

That action often looks like a communication strategy. If all your lessons learned are kept inside of a document no one ever reads, it really has no impact. Communication in this case looks like collaboration on lessons learned, raising awareness in a population that improvements have been made, and then education of those that must deal with those improvements.

Communication is not only internal. There is also a public relations aspect to it. If your brand has been damaged, you also need to focus on external communication. You also want to communicate your lessons learned with your peer group.

It's important to think about preventing the issues that occurred from happening again. You have to do that. You have to plug the hole in the dam so that the water stops. But often, people get too narrowly focused on that one challenge.

They prevent the known breach from happening again, and then they go back to the new normal without assessing the larger picture, without expanding their lessons learned. Improvement should not come just from addressing the problem; it should also come from addressing the system.

It should come from looking at how this thing actually happened.

THE FIVE WHYS

The Five Whys are a way of looking at a problem, peeling away each layer with a series of "why" questions. Let's say there was a physical access breach onto a secured parking area of your building, accomplished by tailgating. You ask, "Why was the person allowed through the door?" Well, they were allowed through the door because they were tailgating.

Why did you think they were tailgating? I saw them. Why didn't you stop them? I didn't stop them because of whatever reason. And you trace it back—why, why, why.

Always, you ask why.

CONSTANTLY CHANGING THREAT ENVIRONMENT

The way we're getting attacked changes relatively rapidly over time. The threats we're dealing with in 2015 are very different from the threats we were dealing with just two years ago. With threats changing so quickly, it can be difficult to anticipate how you're going to be affected. The lesson is that you need to constantly focus on what the current threats are.

The fantastic thing about frameworks is that they allow you to bring prevention and lessons learned into a format that produces actionable items.

Yes, threats will continue to change, but if you can adhere to a framework, you're ahead of the game. If you follow a framework, you'll be a harder target for the bad guys. They'll pass you by because you're a locked door in the parking lot.

For larger corporations, if somebody wants to get at you, and it's a persistent nation, like Russia, China, or North Korea, it is very difficult to keep them out. It can be downright impossible, even if that sounds like doom and gloom.

But for small and midsize companies, the framework will go a long way to prevent you from being a victim of casual or unfocused attempts. You don't have to be bulletproof; you just need to be better than the next small business.

What we are really doing in this book is advocating for small, medium, and large companies to adopt the mentality that operating out of a framework when approaching security concerns is the best possible strategy. It allows you to react as quickly as possible to threats.

If anything we do in this book has helped enable someone to adopt a framework and to adopt this kind of system, then we know we have moved the needle on awareness of the problem. Our work in this book will have been worth it. And so will your time in reading it.

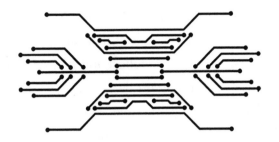

CHAPTER 9

CONCLUSION

The risks to companies from cyber threat are real and ever changing. In order to defend your company and your customers, you need to approach cybersecurity in an organized way. We hope we stated the message clearly in the previous chapters, but there is always a risk of excessive pontification, so we will use this conclusion to restate simply some of the takeaways we hope you get.

UNDERSTAND YOUR STUFF: IDENTIFY

Once you have your act together and understand how your company makes money and how your customers depend on you to be safe, you can move to the next phase: What "stuff" do I have?

Understanding where your important data lives and then gathering information about the devices and systems that hold, transport, or consume that data is the next step. This collection of information can look like anything from a spreadsheet that someone owns to mature inventory policies supported by robust auditing software. Until you understand where your important data is being used and can prioritize that data based on company value, you can't move onto the next phase—of locking it down as tight as you can.

UNDERSTAND YOUR RISKS: PROTECTION

Now that you know what data is important and where it is being used, stored, and transported, you can take steps to protect it. This comes from understanding the threats and attacks that people might use as well as the tools that most people will use to defeat those threats. The problem is that risks are always changing and never go away. The stuff that was being used to attack five years ago is still around. The good news is that smart people are working on the problems and releasing security standards for each of these threats. Working with the NIST Framework and the standards it references is a great start.

My suggestion for small and midsize business owners is to find automated tools or professional services that keep your protection up to speed with the threats that are out there.

UNDERSTAND WHAT IS HAPPENING: DETECT

If you lock the doors to a treasure chest and walk away, you can assume it will be safe forever, right? Hmmm, on second thought, you might want to go look at it from time to time and see if anyone broke the lock open.

The same thing is true for cyber protection. Building a wall but never looking to see if someone is climbing over it makes the expense of the wall a bit ridiculous. We are less and less focused on technology at this point. We now look at processes and procedures to check on that chest in the right kinds of ways.

Look at your priorities around what you are protecting, and come up with business systems—made up of technology and processes—to collect information so that you know what is going on.

UNDERSTAND WHAT TO DO WHEN THE SHIT HITS THE FAN: RESPOND

It's two o'clock in the morning, and your phone is ringing. It's your cybersecurity guy. You've been hacked, and they don't know how bad it is or how it was done. It's actually still happening! What do you do?

Responding to an emergency and 100 percent improvisation are not good partners. While there is no plan that will be able to detail every response to every possible event, you can define high-level policies to help you take action. In our example above, if you see data leaving your network at a fast rate from a particular server, should your team turn it off? What if customers are still using it and you are generating revenue? Are you confident enough in your data? Deciding beforehand what level of response you are prepared to take is key in framing your decision making during a crises.

UNDERSTAND HOW YOU ARE GOING TO PUT THE PIECES BACK TOGETHER AGAIN: RECOVER

You turned your file server off that has all your customers' data on it. There has been a breach. How do you get to the heart of what happened, and how do you take steps to prevent this in the future? These are great questions, and here are a few more:

- How do you tell your customers that you just had a breach?
- How do you reestablish trust in a broken brand?
- How do you work with the authorities?
- Have you called your lawyer? Do you have one?
- Having agreements beforehand with your customers and establishing procedures on what to do is a key part of salvaging your business.

UNDERSTANDING WHAT'S NEXT: HOW DO I START?

Hopefully you have found some good stuff here that will allow you to wrap your mind around what a large enterprise is thinking about when it comes to cybersecurity and have tools now to approach working with them in a way that will keep you both safer. This is a complex problem and one that can seem overwhelming. By breaking it down into sections, you can succeed. You don't have to be a victim. You can be proactive and take control of your responses to the risks.

You can't control what the bad guys are going to do, but you can control your behaviors before and after they strike. Use a security framework and be smart about how you lock your cybersecurity doors.

APPENDIX

APPENDIX A:
TWENTY-TWO WAYS TO LOCK YOUR COMPANY'S CYBER DOORS FOR UNDER 20K

This is a section with our top suggestions for tightening up your small to midsize business's cybersecurity. These suggestions won't keep you 100 percent safe, but they should make it hard enough that the bad guys go after someone else. Think about it like this. If you and I are being chased by a bear, I don't have to outrun the bear, only you.

SMALL BUSINESS:

Twenty-Two Ways to Lock the Doors

	NIST FRAMEWORK FUNCTIONS	SUGGESTION	EXPLANATION
1	Identify Protect Detect	Consider outsourcing your security to a security provider.	You can either be an expert in cybersecurity or an expert in what your company does. You have a CPA, and you have a lawyer. You should also have a managed service provider.
2	Identify	Have a master list of the inventory of your devices.	You can't protect what you don't know you have.

3	Identify	Understand your business model so you can prioritize initiatives. Then act.	Don't boil the ocean. You can't do it all today. A lot of these things won't cost extra money. Do those things first.
4	Identify	Know your data and your customers' data and how they are used.	Set a policy on what data is important to you. Track where it is, and make sure you know who's using it and where they're using it.
5	Protect	Use encryption on your wireless access points.	Make sure you enable encryption inside your wireless access points.
6	Protect	Hide your service set identifier (SSID).	Check the box to hide your SSID. This is the name of your wireless device that you see when you're trying to connect to a Wi-Fi network. This will mean you will have to type the Wi-Fi name to connect to it.
7	Protect	Disable access from outside network.	If your router (wired or wireless) has a Web management interface, disable access from the outside network. And change the admin default password now. Most routers have the ability to do both quite easily. You don't want anyone else coming in and changing your settings or reading your log files.
8	Protect	Use antivirus software and antispyware protection.	Make sure all of your PCs use antivirus software, and if you're using Windows, add antispyware protection. This seems obvious, but it bears restating. While you are at it, check to make sure that all of your antivirus subscriptions are current. Anything out of date won't do you any good.
9	Protect	Use remote web hosting.	For people without an IT background, it is complicated and risky to host your own web services. It is much safer to host it on Amazon, Google, or some other reputable service provider. Make sure you pay the extra money to enable the security features from these services.

10	Protect	Move your file hosting to a cloud provider.	Having a local file server is risky. You have to worry about physical security, fires, and people getting access to it manually. On-line data storage is cheap, affordable, and highly reliable. Only store things locally if you have concerns about your Internet connection.
11	Protect	Disable file/print sharing on everything other than your file server.	File and print sharing is a setting on all Windows devices that helps two computers communicate to each other and share files easily. With today's technology, this sharing is often not needed. This is a tool that malicious people on your network will use to access confidential documents.
12	Protect	Use whole disk encryption on all laptops and computers.	Purchase a software product that encrypts hard drives before the operating system is even started. This will keep someone who steals a laptop or computer from using any operating system exploits to bypass username and password.
13	Protect	Start doing regular off-site backups now.	All it takes is a spilled drink on your laptop to lose everything. Life happens. Back up your stuff today. Use a cloud backup provider, such as Carbonite or Google.
14	Protect	Encrypt your data at rest, in transit, and where it is consumed.	Your data is everything. Make sure you encrypt it wherever it happens to be. This means use SSL everywhere. You can purchase SSL certificates from your web service provider.
15	Protect	Don't forget physical security for your hardware.	It's a lot easier for someone to steal a device than to reach out across the Internet and touch you. Don't make it easier. Lock things up.
16	Protect	Segment your network.	Offer a guest network for Wi-Fi and a private network.
17	Protect	Educate your employees through cybersecurity training.	The number-one security threat you will face is your employees. Invest in training programs offered by third parties. For example, train them how to detect a phishing attack and best practices once they detect one.
18	Protect	Consider using two-factor authentication.	Passwords don't protect anything. Use a second form of identification, such as a cryptographic key or a phone app.

19	Protect	Patch your infrastructure.	This is the number-one thing you can do to protect yourself. Microsoft has wonderful automated patching tools. Enable all automated patching for all software. The good far outweighs the bad with this.
20	Detect	Know who is on your network.	Your routers have logs that tell you who has been on your network from time to time. You should look at these to see if the devices on your network match the devices you trust. For extra safety, you can even define what devices are allowed to connect to these routers.
21	Respond	Have policies in place for BYOD.	If you do BYOD, create policies on how you handle data on those devices and consider implementing a software product to enforce those policies.
22	Respond Recover	Create a plan on what to do if your data or your customers' data is compromised.	Make a plan on how to react before something goes wrong. Chances are, you'll need help with this. Find out what your customers are expecting.

APPENDIX B: HOW TO INCREASE YOUR NIST CYBERSECURITY MATURITY LEVELS

MIDSIZE COMPANIES:

How to Become a Tier 2 or Higher on the
NIST Cybersecurity Framework

	NIST FRAMEWORK FUNCTIONS	SUGGESTION	EXPLINATION
1	Identify Protect Detect	Security is tested with penetration tests and red team exercises	Test the overall strength of an organization's defenses (the technology, the processes, and the people) by simulating the objectives and actions of an attacker.
2	Identify	Inventory of authorized and unauthorized devices	Actively manage (inventory, track, and correct) all hardware devices on the network so that only authorized devices are given access and unauthorized and unmanaged devices are found and prevented from gaining access.
3	Identify	Inventory of authorized and unauthorized software	Actively manage (inventory, track, and correct) all software on the network so that only authorized software is installed and can execute and that unauthorized and unmanaged software is found and prevented from installation or execution.
4	Identify Protect	Continuous vulnerability assessment and remediation	Continuously acquire, assess, and take action on new information in order to identify vulnerabilities, remediate, and minimize the window of opportunity for attackers.

5	Protect	Secure configurations for hardware and software on mobile devices, laptops, workstations, and servers	Establish, implement, and actively manage (track, report on, correct) the security configuration of laptops, servers, and workstations using a rigorous configuration management, and change control process in order to prevent attackers from exploiting vulnerable services and settings.
6	Protect	Malware defenses	Control the installation, spread, and execution of malicious code at multiple points in the enterprise, while optimizing the use of automation to enable rapid updating of defense, data gathering, and corrective action.
7	Protect	Application software security	Manage the security lifecycle of all in-house developed and acquired software in order to prevent, detect, and correct security weaknesses.
8	Protect	Wireless access control	Control access to the network through wireless devices by understanding the processes and tools used to track/control/prevent/correct the security use of wireless local area networks (LANS), access points, and wireless client systems.
9	Protect	Secure configurations for network devices such as firewalls, routers, and switches.	Establish, implement, and actively manage (track, report on, correct) the security configuration of network infrastructure devices using a rigorous configuration management and change control process in order to prevent attackers from exploiting vulnerable services and settings.
10	Protect	Limitation and control of network ports, protocols, and services	Manage (track/control/correct) the ongoing operational use of ports, protocols, and services on networked devices in order to minimize windows of vulnerability available to attackers.

11	Protect	Controlled use of administrative privileges	Control and track the use of administrative accounts by developing and understanding the processes and tools used to track/control/prevent/correct the use, assignment, and configuration of administrative privileges on computers, networks, and applications.
12	Protect	Boundary defense	Detect/prevent/correct the flow of information transferring networks of different trust levels with a focus on security-damaging data.
13	Protect	Controlled access based on the need to know	Control who has access to what data by understanding and implementing a set of processes and tools used to track/control/prevent/correct secure access to critical assets (e.g., information, resources, systems) according to the formal determination of which persons, computers, and applications have a need and right to access these critical assets based on an approved classification.
14	Protect	Data protection	Protect data by understanding and implementing a set of processes and tools used to prevent data exfiltration, mitigate the effects of exfiltrated data, and ensure the privacy and integrity of sensitive information.
15	Protect Detect	Security skills assessment and appropriate training to fill gaps	For all functional roles in the organization (prioritizing those mission-critical to the business and its security), identify the specific knowledge, skills, and abilities needed to support defense of the enterprise; develop and execute an integrated plan to assess, identify gaps, and remediate through policy, organizational planning, training, and awareness programs.

16	Protect Detect	Secure network engineering	Make security an inherent attribute of the enterprise by specifying, designing, and building in features that allow high-confidence systems operations while denying or minimizing opportunities for attackers.
17	Detect	Maintenance, monitoring, and analysis of audit logs	Collect, manage, and analyze audit logs of events that could help detect, understand, or recover from an attack.
18	Detect	Account monitoring and control	Actively manage the life-cycle of system and application accounts—their creation, use, dormancy, deletion—in order to minimize opportunities for attackers to leverage them.
19	Respond	Incident response and management	Protect the organization's information, as well as its reputation, by developing and implementing an incident response infrastructure (e.g., plans, defined roles, training, communications, management oversight) for quickly discovering an attack and then effectively containing the damage, eradicating the attacker's presence, and restoring the integrity of the network and systems.
20	Recover	Data recovery capability	Reliably recover data through a set of processes and tools used to properly back up critical information with a proven methodology for timely recovery of it.

**The 20 items above are classified as the 20 Critical Security Controls for Effective Cyber Defense and were developed by the Council on Cybersecurity through their collaboration with governments, institutions, and individuals. Go to counciloncybersecurity. org/critical-controls to download the entire Critical Security Controls Document.

For more resources on the NIST Cybersecurity Framework, visit www.nist.gov/cyberframework/.

ABOUT THE AUTHORS

ADAM ANDERSON, CEO, PALMETTO SECURITY GROUP

Adam Anderson is the founder and CEO of Palmetto Security Group, an IBM Premier Business Partner that resells IBM software and offers professional services around the IBM Security suite of products.

His experience with Palmetto Security Group and the lessons he has learned through working with large Fortune 500 companies inspired him to write this book and to start a new company, Atlas Vault LLC, in order to provide a tool to those businesses that the big guys rely on in order to get business done.

Early Career

Adam left the University of Utah in 1998, after changing majors eight times in two years. He decided to walk the path of the geek/ nerd, trying to help resolve that Y2K thing with a group of other savvy professionals. He'd like to take all the credit he deserves for averting the end of the computer world on January 1, 2000. Once this mission was complete, he joined a large global retail company, Royal Dutch Ahold, and applied his attention to collecting and monitoring data on the company's IT infrastructure. Still being a punk early twenty-something at this point, he stated to his management, "I'm not challenged enough. Give me something harder."

Gleefully, management responded to his request by throwing Adam into the deep end of the pool, known as IBM Identity and Access Management Security. Two years later, Ahold outsourced a large portion of its IT infrastructure to EDS/HP. Once again, Adam asked management for more responsibility, only to find that the road was now closed. Rather than sit and wait for the end, Adam asked for a letter of recommendation and went to work for IBM as a traveling consultant. He lived as a road warrior for two years, until he realized that all his friends were hotel staff, flight attendants, and bartenders. He knew something had to change when his golden retriever no longer cared if he was home or not.

Entrepreneurial Endeavors

After one eighteen-hour layover in Montgomery, Alabama, Adam decided that if he was going to live this life, he was going to do it his way.

In 2005, Adam started Palmetto Software Group, LLC with one client. He cashed out his 401k and all his investments and floated himself for two months until his first invoice was filled. Through a number of successes and failures he has developed an acute sense of the correct threshold of risk needed to grow a sustainable business. A natural progression of risk awareness for Adam was to mitigate risk by becoming aware of his own limitations and actively recruiting people who could fill those roles in the business. In his opinion, it is working with these people that makes it a joy for him to go to work every day, and through their support he is able to guide the future of this exciting and fast-moving security firm.

In the summer of 2014, Adam changed the name of his company to Palmetto Security Group, reflecting the specific area in which his company excels—the IT security sector, especially identity and access management. It just made sense.

What's Happening Now?

Adam recently became the chief security officer of Ellipsis (www. humanpresence.net), a software company that has developed a technology that invisibly detects human site visitors by identifying specific human behaviors. He is also in the process of starting a new software company, Atlas Vault, around a vendor management software tool. He has seen firsthand what a huge undertaking it is for an enterprise to bring a vendor into their network. It presents huge risk to the company, and more often than not, vendor cybersecurity is just an afterthought in the procurement process. Adam is working with enterprise-level companies to create self-assessments for vendors that feed into an executive dashboard to display vendor information and cybersecurity risk levels. This will help the enterprise mitigate the risk from these vendors and ultimately determine who to work with where sensitive data is involved. This product should be ready for market by the end of 2015.

His primary business passion is with Atlas Vault. With that company, Adam is trying to help large firms answer the question "Who are my vendors, and what risks are they introducing into my environment?" That calling—to help build trust between large business and small vendor—is the driving focus for him today.

Community Involvement

In 2011, the *Greenville Business Magazine* wrote the following about Adam Anderson when they honored him as one of Greenville's Best & Brightest 35 and Under:

In 2005, Adam saw a need for Internet security services in the Upstate and assembled a team of experts to provide Internet security solutions to area businesses. PSG now has twenty employees and serves clients across the United States and Europe. The self-proclaimed risk taker loves kayaking, rock climbing, downhill skiing and the like, but he also enjoys scaling roofs and hammering nails with Habitat for Humanity. Adam was disturbed to find that many veterans were unable to find work after returning home from service, so he brainstormed a company which he plans on launching in 2012 that will train service men and women for re-entry into the work force. Adam sets an example in leadership for his employees. He supports Junior Achievement and allots time for them to contribute as teachers and mentors for the organization as well. He is also a member of the Greenville Chamber of Commerce and GSA Technology Council.

Because Adam's company for veterans did not have the impact he wanted, he recently decided to go down a different nonprofit route by joining Apparo. He believes that organization already has the necessary resources and business capabilities to be beneficial to many other nonprofit organizations, including those that help veteran soldiers. Adam and his employees also continue to work with Habitat for Humanity, Junior Achievement, Goodwill, and many other local organizations. He is the current Clemson MBA Entrepreneur in Residence and is also an active member of UCAN (Upstate Carolina Angel Network).

Adam happily resides in Greenville, South Carolina, with his wife, Kerry, and two kids, Eva and Kenton.

TOM GILKESON, CISSP, CORPORATE SECURITY DIRECTOR, MICHELIN NORTH AMERICA

Tom is an experienced corporate security executive with extensive knowledge in security and risk management supporting private and government activities.

He currently serves as the director of corporate security for Michelin North America, Inc. Prior to his corporate career, Tom served the US government in counterintelligence and law enforcement roles, both domestically and internationally, for approximately twenty years.

Tom graduated from the United States Air Force Academy in 1988. Upon graduation he received his first assignment to Wright Patterson Air Force Base in Dayton, Ohio, where he worked on top secret projects to upgrade SR-71 and U-2 spy plane surveillance features. During that assignment, the Air Force Office of Special Investigations (OSI) took notice of him and recruited him. He graduated from the OSI academy in March of 1993 and began his seventeen-year career as an OSI special agent.

Tom was exposed to many different security and law enforcement disciplines in his early career but settled on counterintelligence and antiterrorism as his focus areas. During his OSI career he racked up extensive experience leading international security and law enforcement operations in Italy, Saudi Arabia, Japan, UK, Kuwait, Qatar, Bahrain, China, Canada, and Mexico.

He also served as the OSI liaison to the FBI, supporting joint FBI-OSI counterintelligence and counterterror operations. Following the 9/11 attack, he supported investigative operations during the

PENTTBOMB investigation and became a founding member of the FBI's National Joint Terrorism Task Force.

In 2004, Tom deployed to Northern Iraq during Operation Iraqi Freedom. He led human intelligence source operations to protect coalition forces and infiltrated and dismantled the black market in man-portable surface-to-air missiles in his area of operations.

In his final military assignment, Tom created and built a counter-intelligence unit to support US Special Operations Command. His unit deployed globally and collected and provided threat information, initiated operations to neutralize threats, and conducted armed protective services in support of special operations.

Tom retired from the US military at the rank of Lieutenant Colonel in 2008 with distinguished honors, including being awarded the Bronze Star for his accomplishments during the Iraq War.

Shortly after his retirement, The Walt Disney Company reached out to Tom to recruit him for their security team. Tom applied his counterintelligence skillset to help Disney build a world-class information protection program, securing Disney's intellectual property and prerelease theatrical content. One of his most interesting challenges at Disney was developing a program to prevent fans of the TV show *Lost* from collecting and leaking plot details (spoilers) prior to air date. His operation successfully protected the plotlines of the last two seasons of the show, including the series finale.

Since 2012, Tom has been responsible for strategic security programs for Michelin's North American business unit. In cooperation with Michelin's executive leadership team, he has developed and executed strategies to assess and mitigate risks; manage crises and incidents; maintain continuity of operations; and safeguard the company's people, assets, and intellectual property.

Tom currently lives in Greenville, South Carolina, with his wife of twenty-three years, Christin, and their youngest daughter, Olivia. Their two older children, Connor and Rachele, are currently studying at university away from home.

Printed in the USA
CPSIA information can be obtained
at www.ICGtesting.com
JSHW012054140824
68134JS00035B/3433